ORNAMENTAL GRASSES

ORNAMENTAL GRASSES

THE AMBER WAVE

CAROLE OTTESEN

McGRAW-HILL, INC.
New York   San Francisco   Washington, D.C.   Auckland   Bogotá
Caracas   Lisbon   London   Madrid   Mexico City
Milan   Montreal   New Delhi   San Juan
Singapore   Sydney   Tokyo   Toronto

First McGraw-Hill paperback edition, 1995

1 2 3 4 5 6 7 8 9 0   DOC / DOC   8 9 1 0 9
1 2 3 4 5 6 7 8 9 0   DOC / DOC   9 0 0 9 8 7 6 5

ISBN 0-07-047933-X (HC)
ISBN 0-07-048021-4 (PBK)

Library of Congress Cataloging-in-Publication Data

Ottesen, Carole, date.
    Ornamental grasses / by Carole Ottesen.
    Bibliography
    Includes index.
    ISBN 0-07-047933-X (hc)   0-07-048021-4
    1. Ornamental grasses.   I. Title.
SB431.7.O88   1989
716—dc20   89-8123
                                                                            CIP

Chapter 8 line drawings by Andrea Ottesen
Book design by Stanley S. Drate, Folio Graphics Company, Inc.
Packaged by Rapid Transcript, a division of March Tenth, Inc.

CONTENTS

ACKNOWLEDGMENTS

Ornamental Grasses grew out of love and enthusiasm for grasses—my own and that of many others: designers, horticulturists, nurserymen, and gardeners, all of whom have enriched its text with their advice, ideas, and experience.

To the busy gardeners, nurserymen, and horticulturists who patiently answered questions and generously shared their experience, I am deeply grateful. Kurt Bluemel carved time out of an immensely busy schedule to make himself available to answer questions and share his expertise—not only of grasses but of their often confusing botanical nomenclature. John Greenlee took a special interest, taking time to explain the problems and pleasures of growing grasses in a dry climate. Norm Hooven allowed me to quote from his well-written catalog. Jim and Joey Peace generously supplied plants. Pauline Vollmer set down a quarter of a century's experience of growing and enjoying ornamental grasses. Mary Hockenberry Meyer and Dick Simon put great effort into their contributions, taking pains to get the information right. John Elsley and Peter Loewer shared both experience and illustrations.

Other contributors struggled to put into words the complex, nonverbal process of designing a garden with grasses. I offer profound thanks to designers Edith Eddleman, Hans Hanses, Wolfgang Oehme, Inge Reiser, and Benedikt Wasmuth for taking time—more than once—to instruct, explain, and illustrate with examples of their work. Where it was necessary to work from afar, I thank Carol Johnston, Sunny Scully, Gayle Weinstein, and William H. Frederick, Jr., for careful attention to the task.

To the growers, nurserymen, designers, and gardeners growing native grasses, meadows, and prairies who offered the wealth of their experience, I owe a great debt. Meredith Clebsch, Cathy Johnson, Judith Lowry, and Joyce Powers shed light on particular areas of native grass culture, while Darrel Morrison was able to comment on the broader picture. Joanna Reed shared insights from her fifteen years of meadow culture. Neil Diboll, with his partner, Brian Bader, took me under his extraordinarily competent wing, generously offering to criticize and edit the text.

To bamboo lovers and growers, for sharing their enthusiasm for some of the most exotic members of the grass family, I am especially grateful. Steve Ray and Gerald Bol allowed me to quote liberally from their information-rich catalogs. Gib Cooper, Todd Mumma, and Robert L. Perry shared the special insight of years of growing bamboo. Richard Waters made valuable suggestions of the most worthwhile varieties for general use, and Wayne Winterrowd offered his unique experience in growing bamboos north of what is considered their hardiness zones.

Thanks to the many who opened up their gardens to my camera, especially to the staff at Brookside Gardens, Washington, D.C.'s, best kept secret. Thanks also to Ryan Gainey, who shared both his garden and his idea of grasses as "an amber wave." Thank you to Annie Thacher, of the Dumbarton Oaks Garden Library, for doing her job uncommonly well, and to Dick Lighty and garden historians Frank Meyers and Mark Laird, for answering my questions on the history of grasses.

Finally, to Sallie Gouverneur and to Joan Nagy, who labored to turn an idea into a reality, and to Bob Oskam, who struggled with an unwieldy manuscript and won, a standing ovation.

OPPOSITE: **The most graceful of all, maiden grass (*Miscanthus sinensis* 'Gracillimus') stands like a sentry in the Maryland garden of Mr. and Mrs. John DuFief. (Design: Michael McCartin)**

ABOUT ORNAMENTAL GRASSES

1. THE HAIR OF THE EARTH

GRASSES HAVE ALWAYS graced the natural landscapes of the earth. Now they are coming into our gardens, bringing sound, movement, lush volume, and abiding color. Versatile ornamental grasses serve in every garden capacity. They are fillers and specimens, meadow and border subjects, screening material and container plants. They belong to no particular style or era but, ageless, embody the ideal expression of each style and every garden.

When they are massed together in contemporary stylized meadows, grasses are absolutely modern. Carefully placed to conjure up the beautiful spontaneity of meadows and country fields, they grow untrimmed, unstaked, and uncut and abstract for our gardens landscapes that are disappearing in the world around us.

Ornamental grasses growing in stylized meadows seem to be the signature plants of a new age of gardening. Yet when they are placed in another setting with different companion plants, when they are repeated at rhythmic intervals within ribbons of annual color, or when they cascade from antique urns, they become fitting inhabitants of a Victorian pattern garden.

When native grasses mix with forbs in a random planting, they take on yet another role. They serve as the backbone of landscape restorations of native meadow and prairie plantings. In fact, no meadow or prairie is thinkable without them. They are the form, the volume, and matrix for the fleeting bloom of wildflowers.

Ornamental grasses perform gracefully and long in a traditional flower border. Besides adding their own showy blooms, they separate and mitigate harsh contrasts in the form and color of other perennials, and they puff up the border with a soft, encompassing green fullness that persists long after other plants have withered into sticks.

In a naturalistic garden, grasses bring texture and softness and nuance that is utterly fitting. Along the edge of a woodland, they are transition plants. Next to a hard mass of rocks and boulders, they are exquisite contrast: pliant and weightless. Overhanging a pond, they are billowy, green accents, mirrored in still water. Even in the smallest Japanese-style garden, you will find a grass small enough and controlled enough to represent all grasses.

Grasses are not new. If they seem so, it is only because we haven't thought of them as ornamentals before. They have always been there, a bit like the girl next door, waiting to be noticed but so obvious they were virtually invisible. Perhaps when we looked at them before, they registered only as familiar and useful vegetation—part of the background but not part of the garden.

It is easy to see why. The relationship between people and grass is as old as agriculture. Throughout history, members of the grass family, *Gramineae,* have provided grain and cereal to the peoples of the world. Virtually every society has cultivated one or more of their number as a staple food. If the type of grain differed markedly from continent to continent—and even from country to country—all of the grains that still flavor the varied and distinctive cuisines around the globe share a common ancestry. The wheats *(Triticum),* ryes *(Secale),* and barleys *(Hordeum)* of Europe, the maize *(Zea)* of the Americas, the brown durra *(Sorghum)* of Africa, and rice *(Oryza),* the dietary mainstay of many parts of Asia, number among the 7000 genera of the family *Gramineae.*

The cornerstone of man's diet, grass family members also season food (sugar cane, *Saccharum);* provide forage for livestock *(Andropogon, Bouteloua, Borus, Festuca, Panicum, Pennisetum,* and others), which in turn provide meat and dairy products; become starches for alcohol *(Hordeum, Oryza, Secale,* and others); and even scent the air with the essential oils of perfumery *(Cymbopogon, Vetiveria).* Other grasses are woven into hats, mats, fences, and roofs *(Arundo, Avena, Phragmites, Triticum)* and provide thousands of useful manufactured articles *(Bambusa, Phyllostachus, Arundinaria).*

In addition to providing forage and food, grasses and sedges (members of the *Cyperaceae* family) are friendly and familiar vege-

Fields of grain are familiar and friendly vegetation the world over. At first glance, these rows of feather reed grass *(Calamagrostis acutiflora stricta)* at the Limerock Ornamental Grass Nursery in Port Matilda, Pennsylvania, look like a field of grain.

Stylized meadows incorporating masses of perennials and ornamental grasses abstract for our gardens landscapes that are disappearing in the natural world. In the Rosenberg garden on Long Island, masses of lavender, blue oat grass *(Helictotrichon sempervirens)*, and Eulalia grass *(Miscanthus sinensis)* join in a flowing, sophisticated meadowlike ground cover. (Design: Oehme, van Sweden & Associates, Inc.)

tation everywhere on the earth. Grasses grow everywhere but in the sea. At nearly every latitude, on every continent, in every country, these plants constitute a large and essential part of the natural landscape. Because they are a soft, downy vegetation that covers the entire surface of the earth, one enthusiast, the German plantsman Karl Foerster, called them "Mother Earth's hair."

There are mountain grasses whose roots have found anchorage in tiny rock fissures. There are grasses growing on the tundras of the far north that spend much of the year under a deep cover of snow. There are even grasses that grow along the mucky edges of ponds and others that grow where rainfall is seasonal. Giants like the mighty Moso bamboo form dense thickets, and tiny miniatures bloom in the low light of the forest floor. On the prairies and steppes, grasses are a dominant and distinguishing vegetation that comprises a unique ecosystem. Elsewhere they are a large and important layer in a hierarchy of plants that steps down from the crowns of the loftiest forest trees to the tiniest mosses and lichens. Their amazing adaptability is a boon to their use in the garden. Because ornamental grasses belong to the most widespread plant families on earth, there is an ornamental grass for virtually every situation.

Roughly divided by their pattern of growth, ornamental grasses fall into two categories. Some, like lawn grasses, are sod-forming, while others are hummock-forming. They are also divided by their seasons of growth. Cool-season grasses grow when the weather is cool, or even cold, and sometimes go dormant in hot weather. Warm-season grasses grow when the weather is settled and warm, going dormant in cold weather.

Within these categories is an enormous variety of colors, shapes, and sizes. There are miniatures suitable for rock gardens, medium-sized grasses for ground covers and border plants, and larger grasses for specimens, screens, and accents. Most are not finicky about soil or water. With the exception of the "running" bamboo and grasses, they are easy to control. They do not outgrow their space or alter light and moisture conditions in the way that trees and shrubs do.

In addition to their ability to fend for themselves, other qualities of ornamental grasses make them perfect candidates for easy-to-care-for, environmentally sensitive, and nostalgic gardens. First among these is their casual good looks. Warm-season grasses have clean, fresh-looking foliage throughout the growing season, with many of them at their absolute peak during and after the hottest days of summer. Insects leave them alone and disease is not a problem.

Those of us who do our own weeding, watering, and planting find that ornamental grasses are maintenance bargains. Because they are good competitors, outgrowing weeds and remaining healthy, their inclusion in a garden actually diminishes upkeep. Unlike lawn, they require no frequent mowing, liming, and weed killer. Unlike many woody ornamentals, grasses grow quickly to their ultimate size; their effect is immediate. If planted in spring, a grass exhibits the appearance of full-blown maturity by fall.

Grasses are excellent choices for an environmentally friendly garden. When native grasses are used for prairie or meadow restorations, they restore precious wildlife habitats that are disappearing elsewhere, providing food for a wide diversity of animals. Deer, horses, and cattle graze on the foliage, and birds and small animals eat the seeds. Native grasses work to stabilize soil and prevent erosion. Once established, they are fully adapted to their sites and do not need fertilizer, supplemental water, or other help to grow. Meadows and prairies are also important gene banks, repositories of botanic characteristics that have evolved over millennia and are preserved in the seeds of native grasses.

Meadows and prairies are excellent, ecologically sound, and lyrically beautiful plantings for large, sunny spaces. Horticulturists call them "climax communities," intermingled groups of plants that come to bloom and seed at different times. As each new group climaxes, the appearance of the meadow or prairie changes.

Meadows and prairies are also the models for stylized meadow-like plantings that suit smaller, residential properties. Because gardens today tend to be small, many of the separate parts and functions of yesterday's gardens—vegetable plot, garden border, shrubbery—are fused into one free-flowing whole that incorporates all of the facets of a garden.

Grasses are ideal candidates for this new garden. When they are added to a garden, it takes on the aspect of the climax community and becomes dynamic. Unlike lawn and evergreens, which are maintained to stay exactly the same all year long, ornamental grasses change dramatically over the growing season. They connect our gardens to the fluid, dynamic processes at work in the natural world.

Along with the forbs, from which the perennial flowers in our gardens are descended, grasses constitute what horticulturists call the herbaceous layer of plants. Herbaceous plants, which die back to the roots in winter, have dramatic life cycles. As they move through these cycles they bring movement into the garden. It changes day by day, week by week, season by season.

As herbaceous ornamental grasses grow, flower, go to seed, and die, they perform in concert with other plants. After bulbs bloom alone in a lifeless landscape in the earliest spring, warm-season grasses quite literally return from the dead. As if by some secret, conspiratorial signal, all at once new shoots quicken and rise above last year's decaying remains. Their re-emergence is dramatic and well timed, dovetailing with the bloom time of flowering bulbs. Grasses grow lush and full just in time to hide the bulbs' increasingly unattractive foliage. With their entrance, the landscape throbs with life; new growth obscures the old.

By mid-summer, grasses are truly astounding in their fullness and density. Growth slows and reaches a steady state, and grasses are at their peak as a lush, neutral filler that buffers the brilliant colors of blooming perennials. Many grasses are late bloomers, providing interest in the late-summer garden when little else is happening.

The sweet-smelling roots of vetiver (*Vetiveria zizanioides*) are distilled for oil in perfumery. Teamed with sunflowers, vetiver grows at the New Orleans Botanic Garden.

Blue *Agapanthus* 'Loch Hope' and yellow pampas grass (*Cortaderia selloana* 'Gold Band') are a cheery combination in the Savill Garden in England. (Photo by Cynthia Woodyard)

Their flowers are often white or buff and do not clash with those of other plants. They are excellent material for both fresh and dried flower arrangements.

Ornamental grasses age gracefully. In fall, a good number of them turn color in the long, reluctant passage into winter. Some colors are subtle and fleeting; others are spectacular. In winter, many grasses turn bright shades of wheat and almond that contrast brilliantly with evergreens, and their mass softens the bareness of the garden and provides cover for wildlife.

Once they are situated in the garden, ornamental grasses are at their best and most decorative when we leave them alone. After planting, we step back and allow them to grow as they will without mowing, clipping, staking, deadheading, or cutting them back— except once each year in the early spring. When thoughtfully chosen and situated, they appear to have evolved in place. It would be easy to mistake a well-chosen planting of ornamental grasses for a serendipitous accident of nature—a few weeds that escaped early detection and have become too pretty to remove.

Grasses endow our gardens with a wild and natural spirit. In the past, gardeners traditionally intervened powerfully and frequently—by cutting back, thinning, and removal the minute foliage withered—and gardens were orderly, manicured, and tame. But by allowing plants to pass through the stages of seasonal metamorphosis, we now garden not tamely, but on the thrilling frontier between designed order and the full exuberance of nature.

The "wild" look is, for some of us, an easily acquired taste that can quickly become a craving. When we choose to garden with grasses, we permit our hold on total order in the garden to relax a bit and we savor a sweet disarray—an ordered disorder. By allowing these plants to express themselves and not intervening mechanically, we greatly reduce maintenance. We garden smarter by working with natural patterns of growth and demise, rather than by struggling against them. Besides omitting much garden drudgery, besides restoring a spirit of the windswept and wild, as maintenance diminishes a sense of fitness and natural beauty is restored.

While low upkeep requirements are a good reason for growing ornamental grasses, far more compelling is the tantalizing natural spontaneity of these garden subjects. It is perhaps because much of what surrounds us is so obviously man-made, manipulated, and unnatural that flowing, blowing, untamed grasses have such appeal. Windblown, carefree, suggestive of prairies and country fields, grasses call to mind a younger, wilder landscape. Natural beauties, they belong in a nontoxic, good-looking, sophisticated contemporary garden.

2. HOW GRASSES CAME INTO OUR GARDENS

Iᴛ ᴡᴏᴜʟᴅ ʙᴇ thrilling to be able to say that ornamental grasses are completely new garden subjects that have been overlooked for centuries and have suddenly been discovered and appreciated for all of their incomparable qualities. But that would be incorrect. Grasses have been here before—not just as grains or part of the scenery, but as bona fide ornamentals.

What is difficult to establish is exactly when they were first transplanted from the field or the physic garden into the garden border and why, for a time, they disappeared.

Picking up the horticultural trail of grains and useful grasses is far easier. History is sprinkled with references to grass family members in their role as plants useful to man. Nearly two thousand years ago, the Roman naturalist Pliny discussed wheat. Six centuries ago, Job's tears (*Coix lacryma-Jobi*) appeared routinely in early herbals; doubtless grown for its hard seeds, which were fashioned into rosaries, it grew in cloister gardens of the fourteenth century. Grains are also well represented in Leonhart Fuchs' *De Historia Stirpium* of 1542. It is a watershed work for its reliably accurate illustrations of plants in a genre in which vague and fanciful illustrations of plants were common. Among the grass family members Fuchs mentions are corn, sorghum, oats, two- and six-rowed

ABOVE: Red zinnias and the annual *Pennisetum setaceum* combined in a summer border at Brookside Gardens

barleys, common millet, pearl millet, rye, and four different kinds of wheat.

During the Middle Ages, gardeners had to content themselves by and large with native plants. Once the voyages of discovery were launched, many of the real treasures brought back to Europe were plants. Probably the first grass family member to be taken from the New World back to Europe was maize, the grain of the Americas. And perhaps the first grass purposefully brought to the New World was *Arundo donax*. Transplanted to California by the Spanish mission fathers, it was fashioned into animal pens, woven into baskets, and grown for protection from the wind.

Plants and seeds traveled back and forth across the ocean—either intentionally or accidentally. By the mid-eighteenth century, purposeful plant exchanges increased. John Bartram, who established the first American botanic garden in Philadelphia, carried on a thirty-year correspondence and plant exchange with Peter Collinson of England. Between 1734 and 1765 he sent Collinson sassafras, tulip poplar, white and swamp oaks, Solomon's seals, hellebores, snake roots, and dozens of other native North American plants. These eventually found their way into the gardens of the nobility. Wealthy patrons also sponsored scientific expeditions to identify, collect, and catalog new discoveries.

In the eighteenth and early nineteenth centuries, cataloging the natural world was the cutting edge of science. Some of the best minds of the Old World traveled abroad to discover and describe the world's flora and fauna. Johann Wolfgang von Goethe, Charles Darwin, and Alexander von Humboldt, who commented on the distribution of the genus *Carex*, were among these. In the New World, John Bartram's son, William, under the patronage of Dr. John Fothergill, traveled into the wilderness, recording what he saw for posterity in his *Travels of William Bartram*, published in 1791. Among his notes are descriptions of stands of native bamboo that once covered thousands of acres along the Mississippi—an "endless wilderness of Canes."

In the face of so much horticultural activity worldwide, it is interesting to note that the first known listing of a grass as an ornamental is not of an exotic. An English native, feather grass (*Stipa pennata*) is listed among flowering plants in the 1782 catalog of Englishman John Kingston Galpine, "Nursery and Seedsman at Blondford, Dorset."

A century later in England, grasses—both natives and exotics—were well established as ornamentals. In 1883, the first of many editions of *The English Flower Garden* by William Robinson appeared. In this work, many grasses, both large and small, are mentioned as ornamentals. Of *Panicum virgatum*, a North American native, Robinson wrote: "Admirable for borders or for isolation in the picturesque flower garden or pleasure ground. Its colour, though quiet, is pretty throughout the autumn, and not without effect even in winter." A few among the many other grasses Robinson mentioned are *Arundo, Gynerium argenteum* (pampas grass), the clump bamboo *(Arundinaria nitida)*, the quaking grasses *(Briza)*, brome grass *(Bromus), Carex pendula* "for shady spots," *Elymus,* Eulalia, millet grass *(Milium), Pennisetum,* and *Uniola (Chasmanthium).*

A scant three decades later, in the first years of the twentieth century, when Gertrude Jekyll was at the height of her designing and writing career, the ornamental grasses mentioned in her works include some of those recorded by Robinson. She situates the big grasses, pampas grass (then known as *Gynerium argenteum*), Eulalia grass, and giant reed (then known as *Arundo phragmites*), near water. Lyme grass *(Elymus arenarius)*—"a native of our sea shores"—is worked into a border of gray and glaucous plants and *Luzula sylvatica* covers a woodland floor.

Both Robinson and Jekyll were influential in the United States, where gardening had grown in status and popularity during the Victorian era. Increasingly during this time, among the specimens collected by plant hunters were plants that became ornamentals. Some of these were specimen grasses that found their way into ornamental gardens. Pampas grass *(Cortaderia selloana)* became the archetypal large grass against which all others were measured. In *China, Mother of Gardens*, plant hunter Ernest H. "China" Wilson wrote of seeing Eulalia grass on the Chengtu Plain: "In places the Chinese pampas-grasses *(Miscanthus sinensis* and M. *latifolius)* are common; in autumn the fawn-colored plumes are most attractive."

Eulalia grass *(Miscanthus sinensis)* served as a stately specimen in purely ornamental gardens. The imposing, dramatic forms and exotic plumes of both pampas and Eulalia grass suited the temper of the Victorian era. It isn't hard to imagine an ornate vase of pampas grass plumes in the same room with a Wardian case and a potted palm.

Smaller grasses were also available. In the John Gardiner & Company (Philadelphia) Seed Annual for 1890, under the heading "Grasses (Ornamental)," there are fifteen kinds of grasses, including the age-old standbys: feather grass *(Stipa pennata),* Eulalia, *Arundo,* pampas, and Job's Tears. Boddington's Spring 1912 Garden Guide lists twenty types of grass seed: the old standbys plus *Agrostis nebulosa, Andropogon argenteus, Avena sterilis, Anthoxanthum gracile, Briza gracilis, Briza maxima,* and *Pennisetum longistylum,* among others. Packets of seeds cost 5 or 10 cents.

In the Luther Burbank Seed Book of 1913 (California), there is another kind of grass, "one of the most wonderful of Luther Burbank's creations, Luther Burbank's Improved 'Rainbow Corn.'

Ornamental grasses were popular inclusions in Victorian gardens. In this photo from around 1900, a specimen of giant miscanthus *(Miscanthus floridulus)*, left, graces the entrance of the Cincinnati Zoo and Botanical Garden. (Photo courtesy of the Cincinnati Zoo and Botanical Garden)

Leaves are variegated with bright crimson, yellow, white, green, rose, and bronze stripes. Rainbow Corn will be the admiration of every one who sees it when planted in your garden. It is something new—it is something desirable . . . 50¢." (Burbank, who pioneered plant breeding on a large scale, fell from grace with his fellow horticulturists for his inflated, sometimes bogus claims—including the breeding of a "spineless" cactus—and his hard-sell advertising.)

In 1930, the Wayside Gardens Company of Mentor, Ohio, offered plants of *Elymus, Erianthus, Eulalia gracillima univittata, Eulalia japonica zebrina, Festuca, Pennisetum japonicum* (fountain grass), and *Phalaris arundinacea variegata* (ribbon grass). Soon afterward, grasses ceased to appear in catalogs. Perhaps they were too strongly associated with Victorian gardens and seemed hopelessly old-fashioned.

One place where grasses lived on was in prairie plantings. While many gardeners looked abroad for exotic specimens to adorn their gardens, a few looked around them. In Illinois, Wilhelm Miller was one of the first native plant enthusiasts in the Midwest, and Danish-born Jens Jensen (1890–1950) championed the disappearing prairie, designing parks and gardens using its native flora. In 1934, Jens Jensen designed the Lincoln Memorial Garden in Springfield, Illinois, whose seventy-seven acres are devoted entirely to trees, shrubs, and flowers native to Illinois.

One of the eight "council rings," circular stone benches for group gatherings designed by Jens Jensen for the Lincoln Memorial Garden in Springfield, Illinois. The seventy-seven-acre garden is devoted to trees, shrubs, flowers, and grasses native to Illinois. (Betty Hulett photo, courtesy of the Lincoln Memorial Garden)

In Jensen's "prairie rivers," grasses grew not as specimens, but on their own terms—in natural plant communities. He recognized that in nature plants are always part of a community that is specific to a region. Jensen found beauty not in the traditional garden styles, but in the restoration or recreation of the natural landscape. Jensen was one of the first prairie enthusiasts, but certainly not the last.

"The first large-scale restoration of a Midwestern prairie was undertaken in the 1930s at the University of Wisconsin under the direction of the great conservationist, Aldo Leopold. . . . Soon other universities, nature centers and wildlife refuges were collecting and planting seeds to establish their own prairies. It was not until the 1970s, however, that many of these plants and seeds became commercially available," notes Neil Diboll in his recent article "Prairie Plants and Their Use in the Landscape."

One of the reasons for the disappearing prairie was rapid development brought about by agriculture on a large scale. The thrust of plant hunting in the United States had been to bring back rare specimens that might prove economically useful. An Office of Seed and Plant Introduction had been established in Washington, D.C., in 1897. One of its agents was Mark Carleton, who set off for Russia in 1898. There he procured the durum wheat strains that were to transform American agriculture. David Fairchild described their effect in his book, *The World Was My Garden*: "Two years after the introduction of the Russian wheats, 60,000 bushels were produced, while only five years later 20,000,000 bushels were grown." The countryside was transformed and "amber waves of grain" became an apt description of much of the American landscape. Agriculture undertaken on an immense scale became a prominent feature of American byways.

As purely useful members of the grass family were being grown on an unprecedented scale, purely ornamental grasses dwindled to almost nothing. Nobody knows exactly why ornamental grasses all but disappeared from the scene after about 1935. By the 1950s, they were difficult if not impossible to procure. If a person in the United States said "ornamental grass," the first thing to come to most people's minds would be "lawn." A few souls, particularly those living where *Arundo donax* had naturalized and where pampas grass thrived, might have considered one or the other of these. But beyond these old standbys and perhaps blue fescue and the odd clump of Eulalia grass, "ornamental grass" was not a common term in the gardener's vocabulary. A few clumps lived on quietly in gardens around the country, but in general, an ornamental grass became a horticultural oddity to some, a weed to others, and virtually impossible for anyone to obtain.

Fortunately, this situation was not universal. In Germany, ornamental grasses enjoyed popularity from the mid-1930s. In the last part of that decade, articles about ornamental grasses appeared several times each year in the magazine *Gartenschoenheit*. A force behind that magazine and the use of ornamental grasses was the outstanding nurseryman Karl Foerster. He spent years collecting grass seeds and plants from America as well as other parts of the world. These he observed for many years in his perennials nursery at Bornim near Potsdam before introducing them to the trade. "The [grass] trials took many long years and were preceded by just as many years of overcoming obstacles to obtain material. On top of that, the hardest summers and winters had to occur before it was possible to separate the good from the mediocre, because mediocrity is poison," he wrote.

Foerster assembled the rich experience of decades of growing and testing ornamental grasses in his book *Eintritt der Graeser und Ferne in den Gaerten (Introducing Grasses and Ferns into the Garden)*, published in 1957. It was one of thirty books and countless articles he published during an achievement-filled lifetime that spanned the twilight years of the Bismarck era, two world wars, and a cold war. Foerster also championed *Schaugaerten* and *Sichtungsgaerten*, demonstration and display gardens for the public observation and testing of new plant introductions. The influence he exerted upon the generation of horticulturists and garden designers who followed

Massed *Rudbeckia fulgida* 'Gold-sturm,' a Karl Foerster introduction, combines with flame grass *(Miscanthus sinensis purpurascens)* and tall giant miscanthus *(Miscanthus floridulus)* at the Brookside Gardens in Wheaton, Maryland. Hans Hanses designed the garden.

him was tremendous. Some of that generation left Germany and brought his ideas and ideals to the United States.

Wolfgang Oehme studied horticulture and landscape architecture at the University of Berlin and came to the United States in the 1950s. It was a time, he remembers, when American landscape architects would set aside a little bit of space marked "flower bed to be planted by owner." He recalls, "There were no plants available—no grasses period. They did a lot of annuals." He had definite ideas about using grasses and other herbaceous plants in garden design but, he says, "I was crying in the wilderness. I had to convince people." For his first commission for a small garden at Goucher College, "I just dug naturalized miscanthus up in the field."

American Richard Simon graduated from Cornell in 1956 and traveled abroad on a Dreer Award. He worked for a time in a Swiss nursery, where he met German-born Kurt Bluemel. Three years later, Kurt Bluemel came to Monkton, Maryland, to work at the Simon family's Bluemount Nurseries. Shortly thereafter, Kurt Bluemel met Wolfgang Oehme, and before long the two easily convinced Simon, already captivated by grasses, to grow them at Bluemount. Before there was any demonstrable interest in ornamental grasses whatsoever in the United States, Bluemount Nurseries offered the first collection of them.

Richard Simon will never forget some of the grasses he imported. Because the European nursery had not washed off all of the soil, he had to drive to the United States Department of Agriculture control station in New Jersey to do it himself before the grasses could be fumigated. Other grasses were obtained locally.

Mr. Bluemel remembers procuring those. "My recollection," he says, "is that Bluemount had *Phalaris* at the time. *Arundo* and *Miscanthus* were all around and we were able to get *Pennisetum* and *Erianthus* from a nursery in New Jersey." The rest came through "digging, borrowing, and buying from gardens. . . ."

After working at Bluemount for four years, Kurt Bluemel started his own nursery in 1964, working for a short time with Wolfgang Oehme. Later, in 1975, Oehme joined ranks with James van Sweden to form Oehme, van Sweden & Associates, Inc. Today, ornamental grasses are this firm's signature plants.

Kurt Bluemel continued to build up the nursery, selling grasses at a time when many people regarded them as weeds. He remembers "being laughed at, being raked over the coals. We are still being laughed at" for growing such unusual material. A newspaper editor friend who visited his nursery saw the vast fields of grasses and quipped, "If you can sell a [pet] rock in a box, you can sell a grass in a box."

Instead of growing just a few grasses, "we grew some thousands

. . . and that showed the landscape designers when they came here," remembers Mr. Bluemel. "They said, 'This material looks quite different when you grow it in huge mass plantings.' It [took on] all of a sudden a whole different aspect—it became a flowering shrub-like plant, a hedge-like plant, a pond stabilization plant. . . .'"

Of the early days of ornamental grasses in the United States, when many people were openly critical of what they considered to be weeds, Mr. Bluemel credits a small group with perservering. "Richard [Simon] was gutsy enough to say, 'I'm going to grow ornamental grasses in this country.' It took guys like Wolfgang [Oehme] and me to use them in public. And Dick Lighty and Bill Frederick were instrumental in recognizing and using grasses [early on]."

William H. Frederick, Jr., is a landscape architect whose firm is Private Gardens, Inc., of Hockessin, Delaware. He was an early ornamental grass enthusiast, using them in his designs in a "mix of herbaceous and woody plants." "My interest in ornamental grasses," he remembers, "was piqued entirely by Dick Simon." Mr. Frederick visited Bluemount Nurseries and saw the grasses that Richard Simon had imported and assembled and soon used them in his own garden.

When in 1968 he was asked to design one of the "gardens for example" at Old Westbury Gardens on Long Island, he thinks it was because "the director knew I would use ornamental grasses." Mr. Frederick lectured on ornamental grasses and found that older listeners sometimes remembered their use in Victorian gardens. He also wrote early articles on ornamental grasses which appeared in *Horticulture* (with Richard Simon, August 1965) and *House and Garden* (August 1967).

Another early enthusiast, Richard Lighty, was in charge of the experimental greenhouses and breeding program at Longwood Gardens when he became acquainted with Richard Simon, Kurt Bluemel, and Wolfgang Oehme in the early 1960s. Attracted to grasses immediately, he began photographing them in 1963 and later used those photographs to illustrate his lectures. In 1967, after becoming coordinator of the Longwood Program at the University of Delaware, he began to bring his students on field trips to the Baltimore-Washington area to visit Bluemount Nurseries, Bluemel Nurseries, and private gardens—including Pauline Vollmer's Baltimore garden, designed by Wolfgang Oehme, which includes many grasses.

Of the Vollmer garden, Dr. Lighty recalls, "Kurt [Bluemel] took me there and Wolfgang [Oehme] took me there and Dick [Simon] took me." To all of them, the Vollmer garden was a vindication of their support of grasses. "It was one of the early things [of which] everyone said, 'This is a good use of the material.'"

Located in the heart of Washington, D.C., the Virginia Avenue Gardens, designed by Oehme, van Sweden & Associates, Inc., have given ornamental grasses a highly visible forum.

Green and white variegated ribbon grasses *(Phalaris)* suit the delicate pink of massed *Astilbe* in this Long Island garden.

On a similar field trip made by Cornell students, Mary Hockenberry, a graduate student, became interested in grasses. Richard Simon sent grasses to her at Cornell, where she studied them and wrote the first publications to appear on ornamental grasses—an information bulletin, *Ornamental Grasses for the Home and Garden* (1973, revised in 1986), and a book, *Ornamental Grasses* (Charles Scribners' Sons, 1975). A year later, Peter Loewer's book *Growing and Decorating with Grasses* was published.

Richard Lighty also took his students to Brookside Gardens in Wheaton, Maryland. In the tradition of the German *Sichtungsgaerten* championed by Karl Foerster, Brookside Gardens, designed by German-born Hans Hanses and dedicated in July 1969, featured sub-gardens in which the new species and varieties were presented in interesting and practical ways for home gardeners. Mr. Hanses describes the gardens as a "series of garden experiences." Generously endowed with innovative, new plant material, Brookside Gardens was the first public garden in the greater metropolitan Washington area to display a wide variety of ornamental grasses.

Brookside Gardens, along with the private Vollmer garden, generated renewed interest in grasses, but it wasn't until 1977 that ornamental grasses had a highly visible, highly accessible forum. In that year, the firm of Oehme, van Sweden & Associates, Inc., was commissioned to design the Virginia Avenue Gardens in Washington, D.C. Located not in a private garden or a suburban botanic garden, but in the center of the capital city, the Virginia Avenue Gardens brought grasses into the public eye.

As ornamental grasses began to grow in popularity, Kurt Bluemel's business expanded. Today, his nursery offers the largest collection of ornamental grasses, rushes, and sedges in the country, to say nothing of perennials, bamboos, ferns, and aquatic plants. What makes him proudest, however, is that he is now exporting grasses to Germany.

When asked why he thinks ornamental grasses have become popular again in the United States, Kurt Bluemel answers that in part, "I should say that we generated the demand. We made grasses popular." In the face of ridicule, he continued to grow grasses, design with them, and promote them while landscape architects like Hans Hanses, William Frederick, and Wolfgang Oehme used them until people finally recognized their beauty. Richard Lighty says simply, "Grasses were an idea whose time had come."

3. GRASSES FOR ALL SEASONS

Grasses and forbs belong to the herbaceous layer of the earth's several layers of vegetation. In a hierarchy that starts at the top of tall forest trees, these layers step down to understory trees—shorter ones that grow in the tall forest trees' shadows—to shrubs that grow in full sun or forest situations, to the herbaceous layer. Nearer the ground, adapted to shade or sun, the herbaceous plants cover the earth like a growth of soft, downy hair—the hair of the earth.

Making up this layer are wonderfully expressive plants. We can look at them and read in their colors and textures and in their flowers and seeds the progress of the calendar. Along with the leaves of deciduous trees and shrubs, plants in this layer are dynamic. They bud and grow, become thick and full, wither and die, and then, miraculously, come back to life again. It is this endless progression of emergence, growth, and demise that defines the grand sequence of the seasons.

The cycles of the passing year have many manifestations in as many different regions. For convenience's sake, we speak of an average year just as we might talk about a hypothetically average man and woman—a person of average height, weight, education, and economic status. In our hypothetical year, it snows on Christmas, the earliest bulbs begin to bloom in January and February,

This carefully planned oval of bulbs, grasses, and perennials in the author's garden presents an attractive and changing vista as the seasons pass. In spring, a burst of tulips follows crocuses that appear soon after the grasses and perennials have been cut back *(left)*. By May, Persian alliums are up and blooming, and grasses again cover the ground *(below)*. In mid-summer, fountain grass and rudbeckias bloom together *(opposite)*. In winter, frost-blanched grass and the dark seed heads of rudbeckias (seen from a different angle) provide seasonally appropriate texture *(opposite, below)*.

April brings gentle rain, July is hot, and in October the leaves turn. This actually happens in some places—sometimes. There are other places that experience no semblance to our "average" year. It may be hot in July, but it may never snow or the leaves never turn or there may not be a drop of rain from April to September. Perhaps it is a place where the seasons only vary from wet to dry. Yet every place has some kind of seasonal rhythm, and plants in gardens everywhere respond to cues in the environment to grow, bloom, and rest.

FALL, LATE WINTER, AND SPRING: COOL-SEASON GRASSES

In spring, herbaceous plants experience rebirth. Some plants, like the cool-season grasses, have been slowly growing all along. In warm winter climates, they may even be evergreen. Unnoticed in earliest spring before settled weather and more obvious rumblings in the earth draw gardeners outdoors, they are, nevertheless, completely revived. By the time spring is official, they have already grown into their prime. All of these grasses are fresh and attractive by the time bulbs bloom. These plants look good and cover the ground and sometimes bloom before perennial plants have even begun to grow. They are in top form, adding richness and delicate bloom at a time when there would otherwise be bare spots in the garden. In very cold climates, some cool-season grasses will stay dormant longer and begin growth only slightly ahead of the warm-season grasses.

So called because cool weather provides optimum conditions for their growth, cool-season grasses may sulk or even become dormant during the dog days in climates with long, hot summers.

Many cool-season grasses bloom very early. Their lacy, delicate flowers are a refreshing entr'acte between the sudden splendor of the bulbs and the rich growth and multiplicity of summer flowers. One early bloomer, *Melica ciliata,* is a small treasure. Even a single plant—barely over a foot tall when in bloom—commands attention at just about the time the tulips fade. Likewise, a number of the fescues peak with great fanfare at the end of tulip season. These pleasant but rather unremarkable-looking hummocks of soft green and glaucous blue never cease to amaze with their size and length of bloom.

A pair of stunning cool-season grasses brighten the early garden with variegation. Stunning white stripes in the foliage of the low-growing, shade-loving *Holcus lanatus variegatus* brighten and contrast with green. Truly unusual is bulbous oat grass (*Arrhenatherum elatius bulbosum variegatum*), the only small variegated grass with a stripe that is blue-green. These variegated grasses also augment the show of early white flowers, azaleas, viburnums, candytuft, and dogwood.

The cool-season grasses included in this book are:

- *Briza media*
- *Calamagrostis acutiflora stricta*
- *Carex* species
- *Deschampsia*
- *Festuca* species
- *Hakonechloa macra* and *H. macra aureola*
- *Helictotrichon sempervirens*
- *Holcus mollis albo-variegata*
- *Hystrix patula*
- *Koeleria argentea* and *K. glauca*
- *Melica ciliata*
- *Melica transylvanica*
- *Milium effusum aureum*
- *Phalaris arundinacea picta*
- *Sisyrinchium angustifolium*
- *Stipa gigantea*
- *Spodiopogon sibiricus*

These cool-season grasses, bamboos, and sedges are nearly or completely evergreen:

- *Carex*, some species
- *Deschampsia* species
- *Festuca*, some species
- *Helictotrichon*
- *Luzula* species
- *Sinarundinaria nitida*

These cool-season grasses "brown out" in hot weather:

- *Holcus lanatus variegatus*. Its white foliage loses its clean, fresh look, and there is die-back at the base, giving the whole plant a dingy appearance.
- *Milium effusum aureum*. The glowing yellow-green color saddens to a drab yellow-green.
- *Melica ciliata*. If located in a hot, dry place, its leaves die back in the center.
- *Hystrix patula*. If located in a hot, dry place, its leaves die back and turn brown.

Cool-Season Stars

Among the cool-season grasses, three superstars perform exceptionally well during early spring, are oblivious to hot weather, and continue looking good far into fall and winter.

Feather reed grass (*Calamagrostis acutiflora stricta*)

Feather reed grass is an ornamental that is above reproach. It greens up in early spring and grows to a foot in height before warm-season grasses like fountain grass (*Pennisetum alopecuroides*) or switch grass (*Panicum virgatum*) show any signs of life. At the end of tulip season, it reaches its full height of about four feet and starts to bloom in foot-long feathery panicles. Flowers last for about three weeks and are followed by narrow seed heads. Of distinctly upright habit, feather reed grass holds it shape well, unless grown in shade, where it becomes floppier. After frost, foliage and bright tan seed heads are showy throughout the winter.

Peerless feather reed grass (*Calamagrostis acutiflora stricta*) makes a good showing from early spring until it is cut down in late winter. After delicate white panicles form in early summer, erect tan seeds adorn the plant for the rest of the year. Here, feather reed grass contrasts with lythrums and purple globe amaranths at the Executive Mansion in Raleigh, North Carolina. (Design: Edith Eddleman)

Blue oat grass *(Helictotrichon sempervirens)*

Blue oat grass is a plant with the "right stuff." Evergreen, it grows about two feet tall with slender, silvery blue leaves arising from a spiky hummock. It blooms in May on long, arching stems that play over the plant, bobbing and dancing in the wind. Flowers are pale blue, turning a bright tan that contrasts stunningly with the blue-colored plants. Blue oat grass is attractive throughout the summer and fall. It is evergreen in warm winter climates.

Spodiopogon sibiricus

Spodiopogon is a grass that looks good from the moment it revives in early spring until the frost arrives. Unlike many grasses, spodiopogon's broad blades are short—under a foot—and are held horizontally on fine, narrow stems. A clump of spodiopogon looks like a small, thick forest of bamboo. Unlike many grasses that always seem to be anticipating their flowers and seeds, spodiopogon looks complete throughout the summer.

SUMMER, FALL, AND WINTER: WARM-SEASON GRASSES

Warm-season grasses stay dormant longer, begin their growth later, and then, after the weather has settled, make up for lost time with a breathless, headlong rush of growth in spring. Frequently, they are at their peak during the dog days and do not bloom until late summer or fall. Many warm-season grasses are also attractive throughout the winter but should be cut back in earliest spring. This yearly cutting terminates the grasses' winter show, which always makes it a difficult task. Once the grasses are gone, the garden is at its most bare.

The bare spots created between the time when grasses are cut back in early spring and the beginning of their own new growth leave just the right interval for bulbs to appear and bloom. When grasses are spaced at least three feet apart, the places in between can be planted with not just one type, but a succession of spring-blooming bulbs. Bulbs bridge the gap between the cutting back of warm-season ornamental grasses in earliest spring and their re-emergence in late spring, when they grow rambunctiously. This spurt of growth is a natural phenomenon that can work brilliantly to a gardener's advantage. It occurs just as the final burst of spring bloom—late-blooming daffodils and tulips—begins a demise. After flowering, the leaves of these daffodils and tulips grow longer and more profuse to manufacture the nutrients for next year's bloom, which are stored away in the bulb.

Bulb foliage always looks messy after the bloom is gone. Acting as camouflage, the warm-season grasses fill in just as the foliage from bulbs has begun to wither and turn yellow. The new growth of the grasses provides fresh new green racing to maturity. It is thus possible to grow great fields of crocus followed by daffodils, followed by tulips, and not have to endure what seems like an endless aftermath of ungainly, sprawling, slowly maturing foliage. Crocuses, narcissus, tulips, and Persian and giant alliums all bloom after grasses have had their yearly cutting back. Each successively blooming bulb draws attention away from the sprawling foliage of its predecessor until the alliums bloom, at which time the warm-season grasses will have begun to fill in. Then the rapid growth of such warm-season grasses as *Miscanthus*, *Molinia caerulea arundinacea* 'Windspiel,' *Panicum virgatum*, or *Pennisetum* quickly outstrips the bulbs' foliage. Evergreen ground cover has long been used to hide or to draw attention away from the bulbs' foliage, but never with the same drama and excitement as grasses.

Warm-season grasses are also good companions to spring-blooming irises, columbines, and poppies. As the grasses develop, they draw attention away from plants that have already bloomed and should therefore be planted in front of, rather than among, these early bloomers. Some versatile warm-season grasses are fountain grass (*Pennisetum alopecuroides*), switch grass (*Panicum virgatum*), sea oats (*Chasmanthium latifolium*), and members of the genus *Miscanthus*, which includes some of the showiest ornamental grasses.

The warm-season grasses in this book include

- *Andropogon scoparius*
- *Arundo* species
- *Bouteloua gracilis*
- *Chasmanthium latifolium*
- *Cortaderia* species
- *Elymus glaucus*
- *Erianthus ravennae*
- *Imperata cylindrica rubra*
- *Miscanthus* species
- *Molinia caerulea arundinacea* 'Windspiel'
- *Panicum virgatum*
- *Pennisetum* species
- *Sorghastrum nutans*
- *Spartina pectinata aureo-marginata*
- *Sporobolus heterolepsis*

HIGH SUMMER

Not only do the warm-season grasses miraculously appear at just the right time, but their own showy progression of many-colored foliage may be used to contrast with, augment, or buffer the colors of summer flowers.

The lush growth of green varieties provides tactful mediation between the brilliant and potentially clashing colors of summer flowers. Grasses like mountain grass or Eulalia grass, in and among groups of perennials, form a lush matrix of buffering green that serves to isolate and enhance the effect of each group of summer flowers. Their voluminous foliage also makes them good filler around tall, angular plants.

When the big grasses—giant miscanthus, Eulalia grass, giant reed, or spodiopogon—reach their full proportions, they radically alter space in the garden. In winter and spring, when the garden is a bright, flat plane of infinite possibility, it is always hard to believe just exactly how large the big grasses will ultimately grow. When they do reach their fantastic proportions, they divide space in a different way, creating a surprising new geography in the garden, with different vistas and secret sub-gardens. Their amazing density, immense volume, and fantastic heights wonderfully confirm the mystery of growth.

But grasses do even more for the summer garden. In the long, hot summer, "there comes a week . . . ," writes Virginia Woolf, "when the year seems poised consciously on its topmost peak; it stays there motionless . . . as though in majestic contemplation." At this time, when the garden rests, grasses also add sound. The slightest warm breath of a breeze shuffles a thousand slender blades. Blade against blade, they bend and tremble, quiver and rush in endless sibilent whispering. Like bird songs, these sounds are fitting and companionable.

FALL

When summer has gone on for too long, when the perennials appear exhausted and bedraggled, when little else is showy in the garden, many grasses still look fresh and have only begun to bloom. Their flowers are elegant, understated, and exotic: silken fans in white and rose, delicate lace on slender, arching stems. Later, when seeds form, there is a great sense of fulfillment. Seeds take many forms but are always suggestive of harvest.

Ornamental grasses are finely tuned barometers of seasonal change. In fall the first barely perceptible changes—a rosy blush, the dry stiffening of seed pods, a slight diminishment of volume—indicate that the slow, reluctant withering into winter has begun. Grass sounds change from soft to raspy whispers. Some grasses, notably flame grass (*Miscanthus sinensis purpurascens*) and *Spartina*, like the leaves of deciduous trees, go out in a blaze of color before passing into winter. Flame grass quite suddenly sheds its quiet green for bright orange-red and holds its snow white, silky flowers dramatically overhead. *Spartina* turns a clear, bright, dazzling yellow. Other grasses are more subtle but no less attractive. The palm sedge (*Carex muskingumensis*) and the giant miscanthus (*M. floridulus*) are briefly and gently apricot-colored. The clear green of fountain

Fall brings a change in this garden's color scheme. Here flame grass *(Miscanthus sinensis purpurascens)* begins to turn color. The bed of threadleaf coreopsis from which it is growing deepens from clear summer green to gray-brown, studded with black seed heads. Later it will turn to thundercloud gray while the miscanthus in the background blooms, then blanches to an almond color.

grass slowly bleeds away and the long cascading blades mottle into a rosy brown before fading to a winter almond.

WINTER

Beautiful as ornamental grasses are in the summer and fall, many people think they are at their best in winter, when their foliage is dry and withered. Most people love to look upon a field of golden grain. Why not plant ornamental grasses, cousins of the wheats and barleys, to light up a winter landscape? Why cut back the dead herbaceous plant when it is the color of a grain field in the fall and winter?

Gardens with winter grasses ought to be planned from inside the house from the place where they will be seen most often. Stake out your tableaux from where you stand at the kitchen sink or sit in a favorite chair. Plant bold masses of grasses to provide glowing winter cover that blends with the taupes and beiges of the dead foliage of other grasses and forbs and is stunning when contrasted with evergreens. Designing with a palette of doves, wheats, buffs, and browns, we can create winter garden vistas that are perfectly suited to the season's subdued light. Using these seasonably appropriate colors, we can plan for the winter garden just as we do for the summer garden.

In a reverse of their summertime roles as quiet companions to brilliant perennial flowers, grasses like Eulalia grass, maiden grass, fountain grass, and switch grass become stars in the winter garden. Soft greens that once served to buffer bright colors become bright

A true giant, eleven-foot Ravenna grass *(Erianthus ravennae)* is a spectacular companion to crimson euonymus. (Brookside Gardens)

Cold turns flame grass to a pale pumpkin color and cotoneaster to a deep maroon at the International Center Garden in Washington, D.C. (Design: Oehme, van Sweden & Associates, Inc.)

Feather reed grass *(Calamagrostis acutiflora stricta)* provides a late winter ground cover at the International Center Garden in Washington, D.C. (Design: Oehme, van Sweden & Associates, Inc.)

shining almond and glowing golden wheat color in winter. However riveting these bright hues may be, they still blend perfectly with the coppers and browns of faded perennials and stand out dramatically against evergreens. There are no mistakes, no clashing colors, only subtle blends and striking contrasts.

The bright winter colors of ornamental grasses provide contrast in a somber landscape. In very large expanses of grasses—meadows and prairie gardens—they can be allowed to contrast with the sky. In smaller settings, winter grasses look best when they are placed in front of evergreens or adjacent to dark masses of perennials like the dark brown seed heads of black-eyed Susan (*Rudbeckia fulgida* 'Goldsturm').

Winter beauty is stark and spare and must be measured by a different yardstick than the one we use for spring and summer. Dried seed heads are not the same as fresh flowers. The frost-blanched papery foliage of dormant herbaceous grasses is stiff and brittle, not pliant and fresh as the living green. When we plant a winter landscape using grasses and perennials, we have to change our expectations and adjust our eyes and minds to a totally different palette of subtle color with brittle, dry, withered textures and the stark angularity of dead organic material. A winter garden is not nit-picking orderly. Nor is a winter landscape particularly neat. It is full of surprises and much of its beauty is accidental. Strong winds shred the blades of grass and snow bends them over. We look at the winter garden through mist, in snow, under leaden skies, and—when the temperature drops—beneath the clearest, bluest skies of the year. To savor the winter garden, we have to accept the vicissitudes of weather and throw away narrow notions of beauty—of a garden as limited to blooming flowers and green and luxuriant foliage. Beauty doesn't succumb to frost. It only changes to subtle, harmonious colors—fields of gold, almond, and tan complementing the dark, stark outlines of trees.

The inclusion of ornamental grasses in our gardens opens up wonderful, new possibilities for an exciting, sophisticated landscape that is spontaneous in appearance. Gardening is always a blend of natural processes and the human penchant for satisfying order. When we garden, we manipulate nature. We select and design in man-made patterns and choices. When we garden with grasses, we do so with a light, not a heavy, hand. The delicate green of spring grasses, their buxom summer fullness, their fall flowering, and the stiff, frost-stricken foliage in winter occur without human intervention as these expressive plants pass through the changing seasons.

Every climate, every season has its own particular beauty. Gardens with ornamental grasses, plants that define the seasons, augment the unique beauty of every landscape.

OPPOSITE: Fountain grass (in foreground), the new 'Morning Light' miscanthus, and evergreens suit the bold stonework of Kurt Bluemel's pool. (Design: Kurt Bluemel)

ORNAMENTAL GRASSES IN THE LANDSCAPE AND GARDEN

4. DESIGNING WITH ORNAMENTAL GRASSES

ABOVE: Massive stone contrasts with 'Skyrocket' junipers and the soft texture of fountain grass at Brookside Botanic Gardens. (Design: Hans Hanses)

THE DESIGN POTENTIAL of ornamental grasses has only just begun to be tapped. As more and more gardeners, designers, and native plant enthusiasts turn skillful hands and appreciative eyes to these versatile flora, we will witness beautiful discoveries and fresh applications for our gardens.

There are so many ornamental grasses that it is difficult to generalize about the group as a whole. Perhaps the one quality they all share is a free spirit. It springs from forms that are loose and flowing, spontaneous and blowing, and it influences every kind of garden situation. In their form is their design function.

It trees with straight, rigid, hard trunks make us think of strength and permanence, and delicate roses on thorny stems conjure up the bittersweet notion of intense but fleeting beauty, then grasses make us think of open places where the wind blows free.

If we try to imagine ornamental grasses as pollarded, standardized, or clipped into topiary, the images that come to mind are ridiculous. It doesn't work. Except when they are completely shorn as in a lawn, grasses are constitutionally incapable of being trained into artificial shapes. They are stubbornly pliant, soft, informal. Yet it is easy to call any number of grasses to mind—*Miscanthus sinensis* 'Gracillimus' and *Molinia caerulea arundinacea* 'Windspiel'

largest selection of ornamental grasses for sale in the United States. (Mr. Bluemel's tips for growing ornamental grasses appear in chapter 12, "Grass Care.") Owner and president Kurt Bluemel estimates that his nursery grows more than 500 different ornamental grasses. His catalog lists 120, and there are more in a gene bank that the nursery maintains—and even more in the ground, growing in row upon row of new and promising selections. Stakes at the end of these long rows bear the names—often musical terms—of potential offerings. Ranging from 'Saraband' to 'Heavy Metal,' the names Mr. Bluemel has given these grasses correspond to traits of growth and appearance.

Currently, Mr. Bluemel is working with about 200 companion plants for ornamental grasses. As befits the bold character of many ornamental grasses, the companions he chooses are not the in-

Blooming fountain grass (*Pennisetum alopecuroides*) in the foreground and *Miscanthus sinensis purpurascens* (with fan-shaped flowers) mingle with maroon Joe Pye weeds, scarlet cardinal flowers, and yellow threadleaf coreopsis in designer Kurt Bluemel's garden.

nocuous "nice-looking little round things that sell very well in a garden center." He is growing large plants with great presence. Among the promising candidates is a dwarf Joe Pye weed (*Eupatorium* 'Gateway') that grows to only four feet but bears a magnificent magenta flower and purple stems. This plant, he suggests, would work very well with *Miscanthus purpurascens*. Some excellent combinations he has found are *Imperata cylindrica* 'Red Baron' with *Alopecurus pratensis aureus*. *Molinia* 'Skyracer' he likes in combination with all colors of *Aster dumosus*.

Spacing, Kurt Bluemel points out, can be "a fabulous design tool." As an example, he says, when using feather reed grass (*Calamagrostis acutiflora stricta*), a grass with strong vertical character, close spacing enhances its verticality. On the other hand, fountain grass (*Pennisetum alopecuroides*), when grown in closely spaced great numbers "would look just like an ocean." Planted farther apart, fountain grass would retain its "hummocky character" and feather reed grass would "round out." Affirming his conclusions is an "ocean" of fountain grasses growing one foot apart at the nursery and, beside it, mounding higher in the center, a handsome four-foot-tall hedge of three rows of fountain grass planted two feet apart.

Hans Hanses

Hans Hanses was educated in Hannover, Germany, where training in landscape architecture includes both design and horticulture. As a young man, he worked in Switzerland under preeminent landscape architect Walter Leder. When he arrived in the United States in the early 1960s, he intended only a short stay—a kind of learning adventure for perhaps a year or two.

At that time, the Maryland National Capital Park and Planning Commission had acquired land in Wheaton, Maryland (outside of Washington, D.C.), for what they envisioned as an arboretum. They were looking for a designer with extensive knowledge of horticulture. Hans Hanses filled the bill.

Nearly ten years later, in 1969, Brookside Gardens was dedicated. A beautifully conceived gem of a botanic garden (a detail of the garden is shown in our chapter opening photograph), it is a treasured local resource that is constantly filled with people jogging, strolling, pushing baby carriages, inspection the plantings, and attending the many tours, courses, and lectures offered there. And Hans Hanses, its designer, is still working in the United States.

"Brookside," says Hans Hanses, "is probably my masterpiece." He remembers that when he began work, his feelings were "against the strictly horticultural type of botanic garden," filled with rare plants of interest to botanists and horticulturists. Instead, he placed his emphasis on esthetics and, in the tradition of the German *Sichtungsgaerten* (where new plant introductions are grown in demonstration gardens to be seen and evaluated by all), he purposely broke away from the traditional notion of arboretum and geared his efforts to "Harry Homeowner," the average member of the public. "I wanted to make something useful," he remembers. For the most part, he used commonly available plants. "People should be able to see [a plant] and go to the local garden shop and buy it." The plants he couldn't resist adding—even though at the time they were not commonly available—were ornamental grasses.

"In Europe we were taught that Mother Nature is the best designer," he says. In nature grasses are a ubiquitous element of landscape. "Grasses," says Hanses, "are the softeners—you soften all planting arrangements with transparent grasses. There is no way you can go wrong."

Mr. Hanses also feels there is "a very intimate relationship between ornamental grasses and other plants, especially the conifers." A favorite combination includes stone, water, pennisetum, and 'Skyrocket' junipers.

He is, however, quick to point out, "I'm not exclusively a grass designer. I'll use anything as long as it looks beautiful. I don't want to limit myself just to ornamental grasses. I don't want to lock myself in a box."

Hans Hanses uses ornamental grasses because grasses are an integral part of any natural landscape and, he admits, "I care very much about esthetics and I'm a big copier from nature. Nature is the best designer."

Wolfgang Oehme

Wolfgang Oehme, horticulturist and landscape architect, is president of the firm Oehme, van Sweden & Associates, Inc., which has offices in Washington, D.C., and Baltimore. His firm is noted both for its strikingly natural-looking gardens and for its use of ornamental grasses. Since he began designing gardens in 1957, Oehme estimates that he has included more than one million ornamental grasses in his garden plans.

One of the first things Mr. Oehme thinks about when approaching a design problem is how "to make the space more natural." After determining "the configuration—what the different subspaces will be," he layers the space, but not in the usual way. Rather than lining plants up from a lawn or terrace with shorter ones in the foreground and, gradually, taller and taller ones behind, as is commonly done in flower borders, Wolfgang Oehme uses multiple viewpoints and layers the entire space so that there are waves of vegetation punctuated by tall, sculptural accents. "I like to have

Above, the flowers of *Molinia caerulea arundinacea* 'Windspiel,' a great favorite of designer Wolfgang Oehme, droop under a heavy dew in the Rosenberg garden on Long Island. Below, the seed plumes of the same plant in autumn. 'Windspiel,' like kinetic sculpture, catches and sways to every current of air. The dramatic change of color of *Sedum* 'Autumn Toy' provides a rich varying texture across the seasons. Yuccas alternately blend in and stand out in the foreground. Low fountain grasses and a mounding spodiopogon occupy the right background. (Design: Oehme, van Sweden & Associates)

something close in," he says, "something right in front of me which forces me to have to look behind it.

"Proportions," he says, "are so important—how you break apart a big area. I think that's where most people fall down. They don't get the scale right." Although he thinks that proportioning space is an intuitive process for him, he does offer a formula for getting the right proportion of grasses in a planting. He thinks it is often underdone; the number of grasses "should be at least fifty percent—this is very important." In addition, there have to be "enough different plants," he states, recalling the "huge, architectural, [homogenous masses] of plants used in the fifties and sixties. . . . At that time, there was no interest in subtlety."

To hold together a design composed of many different plants, he uses repetition. "By repetition throughout the garden, grasses serve as a unifying element."

The gardens he designs are gardens for all seasons. In spring, before the grasses revive, "I plant things you can see from inside through the window. It has to be close to the house." He favors "lots of bulbs" and witch hazels (*Hamamelis mollis*) rising out of beds of herbaceous plants. "Later," he says, "you want to make a certain impact with big grasses. They can be close to the house, too." In his gardens, "the grasses are the highlights." They can either "be big grasses or big areas of smaller grasses." Highlights, however, should not be overdone. "I think," says Mr. Oehme, "it's almost like placing sculpture to have the right effect."

For winter interest, he counts on the presence of ornamental grasses. "Some grasses," he admits, "are better than others. Spodiopogon, unfortunately, is not much in winter; it's there, but doesn't make a show. Its flowers disappear." Other grasses can be effective, he thinks, even if they are not especially durable. One example is the giant miscanthus (*Miscanthus floridulus*). "Even if the leaves blow away," he says, "you get the canes, and they make a statement." In winter, "we use evergreens to have something to hold your eye. Even lower-growing plants like yucca and liriope," used in multiples, function this way.

As accent plants, Mr. Oehme likes the moor grasses and recommends *Molinia caerulea arundinacea* 'Windspiel' and *Molinia caerulea arundinacea* 'Transparent.' While they are enormously effective for vertical emphasis—"like sculpture"—their spectacular flowers and seeds are so finely structured that they are almost transparent. He also likes spodiopogon and the big clumps of miscanthus: maiden grass (*M. sinensis* 'Gracillimus') and porcupine grass (*M. sinensis strictus*). These are "the stars." Other smaller grasses that can be used in masses, such as fountain grass (*Pennisetum alopecuroides*) and switch grass (*Panicum virgatum*), he finds attractive but calls "the workhorses."

Another great favorite is clump bamboo (*Sinarundinaria nitida*). He especially appreciates it in the early spring. "That's when you really notice it. Nothing else is really outstanding. The trees haven't leafed out yet, but the *Sinarundinaria* is bright green and so fresh-looking." Clump bamboo, an evergreen, is also valuable in the winter: "In the snow, it looks like it has been heaped with powdered sugar."

He concerns himself more with texture than with color: "I don't think about color. With grasses you don't have to worry about the color. You can separate it." A favorite combination for texture is using yucca, sedum, and spodiopogon with other grasses.

He sums up his design approach as "a combination of the command of space and good horticulture." The former is largely intuitive. The latter is the result of years of experience. "All my life I've been looking at plants and thinking about how to use them better. You have to know a plant and how it will develop over a period of time—how the plant will look in four to five years, in ten years and, also, how it will look from April to June. . . . One has to experiment with plants to know what looks good.

"We are using groups of plants [perennials and grasses] not considered landscape plants by the profession as our main theme in planting design. These plants create a certain ambience that people seem to respond to and enjoy. . . . Instead of having these plants in a remote botanic garden, we bring the garden experience to people where they are, where they pass, where they work."

Benedikt Wasmuth

Benedikt Wasmuth credits twenty years of growing up in a large perennial garden with his interest both in grasses and gardening. After two years of practical education, he studied landscape architecture at a division of the Technical University of Munich, located outside Munich at Muenchen-Freising-Weihenstephan. In April 1982, as part of a requirement to take "one more international trip" to finish his studies, Mr. Wasmuth visited the United States.

Contacts made on his first visit led to an internship in the summer of 1983 with the landscape architectural firm of Oehme, van Sweden & Associates, Inc., which was then working on the design of the German-American Friendship Garden in Washington, D.C. He returned the following January and in 1985 went into business for himself. He has become known as a talented young designer who uses grasses as part of a sophisticated palette of plants.

Mr. Wasmuth describes his internship with Oehme, van Sweden & Associates, Inc., as "an invaluable experience from a business standpoint." Designwise, he says, the experience helped him to

Easy and green ornamental grasses (front to back): fountain grass *(Pennisetum alopecuroides)*, sea oats *(Chasmanthium latifolium)*, and maiden grass *(Miscanthus sinensis* 'Gracillimus') line the driveway of a Bethesda, Maryland, garden leading to the owner's studio. (Design: Benedikt Wasmuth)

"loosen up" and be "more open to unusual combinations that can be marvelous."

Now that he is working on his own, he says he uses grasses "not only for the texture of the grasses themselves, but for their surprising effects. I use *Molinia caerulea arundinacea* 'Windspiel,' for example, mainly to show the air and its gentle movement."

Grasses, says Mr. Wasmuth, play an important role in the transition from one part of the garden to another. He structures space in a garden "with a rhythm composed of plants that you want to be dominant. Very tall grasses must be free-standing. For example, a *Molinia* between things six feet tall gets lost. You need space to show off its beauty."

"Grasses are essential because of their lush textures," he feels, and the way they combine with other material. "Very often you find colors that you feel you cannot combine—like orange and pink. When you add grasses, they make a harmonious bouquet." He feels

45

that grass should be added to areas "where we usually are reluctant to do it—like vegetable gardens or with roses." He likes the combination of 'White Iceberg' rose with pennisetum and, in shade, the combination of *Chasmanthium* with begonias.

In the gardens he designs, he favors "different focal points in different seasons." He finds that grasses serve as superb transitions and combinations as the focal point moves from one seasonal highlight to the next. "We just don't do enough for the mid- to late summer and fall garden," he says. For late summer and fall interest, he combines "*Helictotrichon* with very low, very deep red *Sedum* 'Ruby Glow.'" To these he may add *Nepeta, Caryopteris,* or *Perovskia.*

"Another season that is completely neglected is the winter," he says, and suggests using witch hazel, winter jasmine, and hellebores underplanted with *Ophiopogon* in places that "you pass every day."

"The most important feature of a well-designed garden is that you don't see the hand of the designer." Plants should co-exist in a "symbiosis, with a peaceful, friendly neighborhood between them," says Benedikt Wasmuth. To such a garden, grasses add an "element of lushness and elegance."

GRASSES IN COMBINATION

Many gardeners find excitement in the way grasses combine with other ornamentals. The potential combinations are almost infinite, ranging from the subtle to the dramatic. Especially for that grand exercise in the art of combining plants, the herbaceous border, do ornamental grasses provide spectacular raw material.

Edith Eddleman

A garden designer based in Durham, North Carolina, Edith Eddleman always uses ornamental grasses to grace her garden borders. Her first design teacher, she says, was Thalassa Cruso, whose book *Making Things Grow* discusses the notion of staging plants and combining them for effect. Formal study came later under John Brookes in England and under M. E. "Tracy" Traer and J. C. Raulston at North Carolina State University, where Professor Raulston had amassed a fine collection of ornamental grasses.

"Grasses have been here before," she says. "I've seen miscanthus and *Arundo* in old, old gardens." Ms. Eddleman grew up "aware that things other than pampas grass existed." She remembers seeing *Arundo donax variegata* in everybody's back yard in North Carolina. Later, she traveled and saw the grass collection at Wisley, which she remembers being "not that interesting all grouped together." She also became familiar with the collection at the North Carolina State Arboretum, but it wasn't until she hit upon mixing grasses with perennials that they truly excited her.

"Gardens need grasses to lift them up and out and above themselves," says Durham, North Carolina–based designer Edith Eddleman. Here grasslike *Liriope spicata* serves as a ground cover in right foreground, while a large clump of switch grass (*Panicum virgatum*) rises up above a stone terrace as a softening specimen. Behind the pool is a well-grown porcupine grass (*Miscanthus sinensis strictus*). (Design: Edith Eddleman)

"I thought if I could take these [grasses] and put them together with other things the way you see them together with other things in flower on the roadside . . . smartweed and purple top and broomsedge. . . . I get a lot of my inspiration from the roadside, and I've always liked the texture of grasses."

Ms. Eddleman was still a student at North Carolina State when her design for a border using a stunning mixture of grasses and perennials was chosen for the arboretum in fall 1982 and implemented the following spring.

"Since the arboretum border was first done, I've done things to enhance it," she says. Frequently, the addition is a refinement in the color scheme. Favorite combinations are built around compatible colors. One combination she has tried and enjoyed is an artful mixture of the pink-blooming shrub *Lespedeza thunbergii*, *Boltonia asteroides* 'Pink Beauty,' purple coneflowers (*Echinacea purpurea*), a pale yellow form of *Anthemis tinctora*, and foxtail grass (*Calamagrostis arundinacea brachytricha*), whose foxtails emerge lavender-colored in early fall.

Calamagrostis acutiflora stricta (feather reed grass) she describes as "my all-time favorite. I like its narrow habit. I like the fact that it's vertical. It's a real exclamation point. You can see through it." Its panicles are "an incredibly beautiful pink-beige color." She likes to combine feather reed grass with *Lythrum* 'Morden Pink.'

In her own garden she enjoys the combination of the bronze-colored New Zealand sedge (*Carex buchananii*) underplanted with "green and gold" (*Chrysogonum virginianum*), cream variegated periwinkle, and pale yellow crocuses and backed by *Mahonia* and a pale cream form of *Kerria japonica. Milium effusum aureum*—"really yellow in spring"—and *Hosta fortunei aureo marginata* form another happy combination in her garden.

Ms. Eddleman uses large grasses like *Erianthus* and *Miscanthus floridulus* and *Arundo donax* to "break the space so not everything is visible at once." But these giants are too large to work in everybody's garden. As a result, she says, "I'm beginning to lean more and more toward some of the smaller grasses for their dainty, airy texture."

"Gardens need grasses to lift them up and out and above themselves," she affirms, adding, "My garden goes through an awkward stage when everything is four feet tall. Then the grasses lift up above that. Gardens have top to bottom layers in addition to layers back to front." The upper layers shouldn't just be "trees and shrubs, but things that are rooted in the ground and fly up above the surface."

Edith Eddleman appreciates grasses' long season of show. "A lot of things look tired and you can't wait to cut them down." But not grasses, she says. "I hate to cut them down."

"I don't like gardens without grasses," she admits, "but I like them as you see them in nature: sporadic, not deliberate. I think of grasses as the thread with which I stitch the tapestry of the garden together."

GRASSES PURE

Some gardeners are captivated by the way in which grasses can be made to combine with each other. The contrast of grass against grass, as in the all-grass border at Planting Fields Arboretum in Oyster Bay, New York, gives added dimension to their use as ornamentals.

Carol Johnston

Carol Johnston is curator of the herbarium at Planting Fields Arboretum, where she has been on the staff for twenty years. She had been interested in wild grasses for a long time and has worked at identifying them for a decade. Displays at the Botanic Garden in Munich, Germany, and at the Pepsico grass garden in Purchase, New York, excited her about the possibilities of ornamental grasses.

When she designed a sixty-five- by twenty-foot grass border at

Planting Fields Arboretum, she found that grasses are in "look and habit very different from trees and shrubs." They are "graceful, almost poetic, as they move in the wind. They look good with other herbaceous material or by themselves." Grasses that do well in the arboretum's Zone 6B–7A climate are "*Calamagrostis, Eragrostis, Festuca, Elymus, Hordeum, Miscanthus, Panicum, Pennisetum,* and *Phalaris.*"

One thing Carol Johnston learned at Planting Fields is that "most of the ornamental grasses we planted do need well-drained soil; some declined in a clayey section of the garden."

Her experience with the grass border has taught her that "perennial grasses increase in beauty as the season progresses." In the border at Planting Fields are several varieties of *Miscanthus sinensis*—'Silver Feather,' an early-blooming grass; porcupine grass with its gold banded foliage; variegated miscanthus; and 'Gracillimus.' Running through the border is a spine of *Calamagrostis acutiflora stricta, Panicum, Stipa gigantea, Eragrostis,* and *Cortaderia selloana* 'Pumila.'

The grass border at Planting Fields is a display that is attractive "for at least three seasons of the year. Many [grasses] look their best in September and October. Tan to brown leaves and inflorescences add winter interest."

GRASSES PIVOTAL AND ENDURING

Some gardeners, notably horticulturist John Elsley and artist Inge Reiser, have created gardens of great charm with ornamental grasses as enduring and pivotal elements. In John Elsley's South Carolina garden, where a hot climate severely curtails the flowering period of many other perennials, grasses are a constant source of color. In Inge Reiser's garden, where clean, spare lines are the rule, grasses function all season long as lush softeners. In both gardens, grasses are dominant design elements to which other plants relate.

John Elsley

John Elsley, who trained at the Royal Botanic Garden at Kew and the University of Leicester in England, is currently director of horticulture of Wayside Gardens and grows ornamental grasses in his own garden in Greenwood, South Carolina. When asked about his favorites, he had a hard time choosing only one or two. His favorites number twelve:

☐ *Briza media*
☐ *Calamagrostis acutiflora stricta*
☐ *Carex conica variegata*
☐ *Carex morrowii aureo-variegata*

☐ *Carex stricta* 'Bowles Golden'
☐ *Hakonechloa macra aureola*
☐ *Helictotrichon sempervirens*
☐ *Imperata cylindrica* 'Red Baron'
☐ *Miscanthus sinensis* 'Morning Light'
☐ *Miscanthus sinensis condensatus*
☐ *Miscanthus floridulus*
☐ *Stipa gigantea*

The front of the Elsley house is the sunniest part of the property. Here is planted a mixture of ornamental grasses and sun-loving perennials. Showy *Stipa gigantea* rises out of a bed of *Vinca*, and the big grasses giant miscanthus (*M. floridulus*) and *Miscanthus sinensis condensatus* are bold but neutral green companions to bright *Rudbeckia* 'Goldsturm.' Closer to the house, shade-loving *Carex morrowii aureo-variegata* is a cool, cream-colored ground cover under trees and edging beds.

Most of the back garden lies in the shade of tall oak trees. Beneath these, Mr. Elsley has assembled a choice collection of shrubs, small trees, and herbaceous plants.

Throughout the garden, groups of variegated hostas and bright bunches of *Hakonechloa macra aureola*, *Carex morrowii aureo-variegata*, and Bowles Golden grass (*Carex stricta* 'Bowles Golden') serve as luminous ground cover. When viewed from the deck, these golden plants have the effect of splashes of sunlight on the garden floor.

When placing ornamental grasses in the garden, John Elsley advises that the garden "isolate variegated subjects for best effect. Try to plant in bold groups (exceptions are larger specimens)," he suggests, because "odd plants are far less effective in display." Finally, in caring for ornamental grasses, he recommends a little coddling. Although grasses are drought-tolerant as a rule, "good growing conditions will enhance growth and hence ornamental display."

Inge Reiser

Inge Reiser, artist and gardener, thinks the reason that we may have overlooked grasses in the past is because they are "so ordinary, so basic. It is wonderful to look at something ordinary in another way." She chose grasses and bamboo instinctively in the creation of her first garden in Potomac, Maryland.

"My garden," she says, "puts me in touch with myself. That's why it's important for me to do it myself—not some landscaper."

Although grasses were around while she was growing up in her native Germany, she says, "you [saw them] more in public places.

Red geraniums (not visible here), roses, and red canvas in the umbrellas and chair covers add the strong color in Inge Reiser's garden. Ornamental grasses in the foreground are green and variegated Eulalia grasses. Mrs. Reiser values their year-round presence. (Design: Inge Reiser)

Land was so valuable, people used it for growing vegetables first." Her warm feeling for grasses comes more from "memories of meadows."

When she designed her garden, she didn't work from a diagrammed layout but from a "picture in my head. I think a garden has to be very planned so that you can let it go a little bit." Designing the garden was, for her, not the difficult part. "I knew," she says, "where I wanted things." The real question was, "Would they grow here? I had not the experience."

Although she greatly admires Japanese gardens with their "green, green, green," she knew herself well enough to realize that she needed some other color. She added her favorite orange-red, "the only strong color I can stand," by adding it in permanent elements—umbrellas and pillows—and in fleeting red roses.

"The first rose," she says, "is so exciting. And picking the last one is sad." But, like the umbrellas and pillows, grasses are steady elements. She observes that with grasses "it's a continuation. It's still very nice when everything is dead. I cut it [back] in April and see already the new green growing. Grass is there all year around . . . like a good friend."

GRASSES AS PART OF THE BIG PICTURE

Appreciative of the fact that grasses add subtle accents and fine texture to a planting, some designers use them as a small part of the big picture, the total landscape that includes trees, shrubs, and

51

herbaceous plants. To William H. Frederick, Jr., and Sunny Scully, grasses are a valuable part of a larger plant palette. They are grace notes that complement and contrast with other plants.

William H. Frederick, Jr.

William H. Frederick, Jr., whose firm Private Gardens, Inc., is located in Hockessin, Delaware, was asked in 1968 to design one of the "gardens for example" at Old Westbury Gardens on Long Island. He remembers including *Pennisetum alopecuroides*, *Miscanthus sinensis* 'Gracillimus,' and *Arundo donax*—at that time, very unusual material. "Most of it," he says, "is still there."

Although he uses grasses "with great enthusiasm," one thing Mr. Frederick feels strongly about is "using grasses as part of a total picture. . . . I'm not terribly keen on having all grasses," he says. "An all-grass garden would be just as boring as one composed only of dwarf conifers. But grasses are very valuable and useful. I like a mixture of herbaceous and woody plants." In his designs, grasses are sometimes used sparingly as accents and, at other times, in great masses.

Mr. Frederick believes that grasses, like other perennials, need division "every once in a while to perform well. With pennisetum and miscanthus, you have to divide every three years for the best effect."

From his viewpoint, "there are two big virtues of ornamental grasses. They really do give you a fine texture you can't get from anything else, and you get an immediate effect. Plant them in spring and you've got a full-blown effect in the fall."

Sunny Scully

Sunny Scully, a principal in the firm of Mortensen, Lewis & Scully, of Vienna, Virginia, began her long association with grasses while still a student of landscape architecture at the University of Wisconsin. There she worked on prairie restorations. Grasses in a prairie are in their native habitat, she explains, adding, "It's a subtle type of landscape." The people who would most appreciate this understated kind of landscape design she describes as "particularly sensitive. It's not for everybody."

Nor does she think that an all-grass design is appropriate everywhere—especially not on the East Coast. "It's a little forced when used out of context," she says. "As you drive down the street, the landscaping shouldn't shock you. It should have a sense of fitting into its surroundings."

She prefers a more gentle approach, with grasses as "only one part of a plant palette. . . . I don't think about just designing with

Grasses are a grace note, a small but beloved part of designer Sunny Scully's plant palette. In the Maclean, Virginia, Steiger Garden, ornamental grasses *Miscanthus sinensis* 'Gracillimus' and *Calamagrostis acutiflora stricta* grow in concert with perennial sedums and evergreens. (Design: Sunny Scully)

grasses. Grasses alone are not that much more interesting than all shrubs or whatever. . . . When designing gardens with impact throughout the year, I'm aware of not only the colorful fall grass, but the after-winter effect when grasses are mowed down. Good designs should accommodate the need for alternate focus at certain times of the year."

Ms. Scully admits, "I certainly have my favorites . . . miscanthus and pennisetum." She likes these two "because I find them interesting structurally. They're elegant with strong architectural form. They can stand alone or mass beautifully."

Although all grasses "have their uses," some are more difficult to use than others, she cautions. "A number are a bit messy. Everybody doesn't want that look." One place where Ms. Scully finds the wild, spontaneous look of certain grasses beautifully appropriate is in the transition between cultivated spaces and natural woodland or meadow. "If you just stop mowing at the edge of a meadow, it can look messy. Ornamental grasses add structure to the edge of the border. You can mass pennisetum adjacent to the lawn, and the meadow will flow behind it.

"Edges are lines that the eye follows. Therefore making the edges read in a strong manner strengthens the design. The placement, movement, and definition of edges are what create excitement in the design." Some grasses that Ms. Scully finds work well at the edge of a forest are *Molinia, Spodiopogon,* and *Deschampsia.* "They mass well, combining softness with character."

Sunny Scully is one of a number of designers who have consistently used grasses in their landscapes. Yet she never sets out to make grasses the main feature of her designs. Rather, she adds grasses to a landscape where she feels they are called for, where they are appropriate, and as "a grace note." She concludes, "Very few plants have the whimsy and response to wind that grasses bring to a planting. They make a garden sing."

GRASSES FOR THE DRY WEST

In climates where rainfall is seasonal, water to irrigate thirsty, moisture-loving garden subjects is becoming both more expensive and less available. In the future, drought-tolerant grasses will play increasingly prominent roles in dry-climate gardens. Gayle Weinstein and John Greenlee grow grasses in the American West and Southwest, where summer can be relatively or absolutely dry. Their experience highlights the need for drought-tolerant ornamental grasses in those areas, which may spur the development and introduction of more drought-tolerant native varieties for garden use there.

Gayle Weinstein

The Denver Botanic Garden is a good place to see grasses—both in the Plains Garden, where grasses native to the Denver area are grown, and in the display gardens, which include annual and perennial ornamental grasses. Gayle Weinstein is botanist, horticulturist, and director in charge of plant collections at the Denver Botanic Garden. Trained in Ohio, where woody ornamentals dominate, she found the scene in Denver completely different. Although gardeners often continue to plant woody ornamentals from other climates in their gardens, it is grasses, along with composites, legumes, and other perennials that dominate Denver's natural landscape.

"The challenge," she says, "is to establish a more adaptive community of plants for this area. Grasses, especially, flower and go to seed and require little water once they have gone to seed." Native grasses are displayed in the Plains Garden, which includes a short grass, medium, and tall grass prairie. There are displays of

Delicate pinks, creams, and whites make up a border at the Denver Botanic Garden that includes the annual fountain grass *Pennisetum setaceum*, pink-flowering *Rhynchelytrum*, white *Nicotiana*, and *Alternathera*. (Photo: John Greenlee; design: Gayle Weinstein)

great interest to home gardeners. One features drought-tolerant mosquito grass (*Bouteloua gracilis*), a superb candidate for a dry-climate lawn grass, in both its shorn and natural forms.

Ms. Weinstein has also used ornamental grasses throughout the Botanic Garden. "The grasses we use ornamentally are not necessarily natives," she explains, "and may include *Miscanthus, Molinia, Deschampsia, Holcus, Lagarus, Pennisetum,* and *Imperata* as well as our natives of *Sorghastrum, Bouteloua,* and *Panicum.*

In recent years ornamental grass displays have dominated the borders. One of these—in pink and white—mixed white *Nicotiana,* the pink-flowering grasses *Pennisetum setaceum* and *Rhynchelytrum,* and *Alternathera.* Another combined *Euphorbia, Pennisetum, Vinca,* and *Holcus* in an all-white garden.

John Greenlee

John Greenlee is a designer, horticulturist, and nurseryman who has grown ornamental grasses for years in Pomona, California, where the southern California climate plays an enormous role in garden design. As in the East, there may be freezes, leaves that turn in fall, and deciduous plants, but for five to six months each year there is absolutely no rain. During that time gardens have to be irrigated to stay green.

"In the West you only get green by adding water." Because green in the West in summer is hard to come by, grasses that "don't do much but be green" have "great value just for adding green to the palette," explains Mr. Greenlee. He lists *Sesleria, Carex, Luzula,* and green fescues like *Festuca muelleri* as good providers of green.

"In the West," says designer and nurseryman John Greenlee, "you only get green by adding water." Green fescues like *Festuca muelleri* are good providers of green. In John Greenlee's garden, it is combined with red Japanese blood grass (*Imperata cylindrica* 'Red Baron'). (Design and photo: John Greenlee)

Green grasses that are also drought-tolerant are the plants of the future. *Bouteloua gracilis* is a very promising lawn substitute that gets by with very little irrigation. Ornamental grasses that Mr. Greenlee recommends as drought-tolerant are *Stipa gigantea, Panicum, Spartina, Miscanthus sinensis, Andropogon,* and *Elymus.* (See John Greenlee's tips for growing grasses in chapter 12, "Grass Care.")

Another approach to gardening in the West is to take advantage of the subtle and unique color palette of the Western landscape. "Brown is a color in the garden, too," says Mr. Greenlee. "People try to duplicate that all-encompassing Eastern green and pass up on rich silvers and browns and rust colors—the natural colors of the hills of California." The hills, of course, are covered with native plants and grasses that require little if any irrigation.

"If people want to get involved with native grass, they will have to get involved with brown. Browns, beiges, and tans are the colors of the stipas and fescues and other native grasses in dormancy. The actual landscape in summer in the Southwest is naturally pale with the colors of these dry grasses and those of other native plants. Any plant that will maintain chlorophyll production in the dry summer in the West will be gray, silver, or dull green."

Because many native California grasses will rot if watered in the dry season, they cannot be grown together with plants that need occasional irrigation. Mr. Greenlee looks to the future when grasses originating in climates with occasional summer rains will be discovered and developed as ornamentals. "The Germans did work with native American things," he says. "Maybe Americans will come up with new varieties of some of our own things. The best is yet to come."

POINTERS ON DESIGNING WITH GRASSES

Placement of Ornamental Grasses

☐ Grasses with fine flowers and seeds need a plain background for their blooms to show up. These include *Deschampsia, Molinia, Spodiopogon.* Place them where they can be viewed against a solid wall of evergreens, a plain fence, or against the sky.

☐ Place large specimens as carefully as sculpture. Allow plenty of space around a sculptural specimen to rest the eye and eliminate visual competition.

☐ Plan for textual contrast by juxtaposing groups of plants and masses of grasses. Texture is enhanced by the repetition.

☐ Plan for the wonderful, enduring volume of grasses. Use these volumes to stop the eye and to create sub-spaces within the garden. Set aside enough space for generous growth.

☐ Plan for movement and sound.

Seasonal Appearance and Behavior of Ornamental Grasses

☐ Consider that grasses' appearance is fluid and changing. Plan ahead for the way the grass will look in all four seasons.

☐ Count on grasses to retain volume after frost.

☐ Combine cool-season grasses with plants that hold the fort during the dog days. Put cool-season plants in places that are bare in spring.

☐ Use succession planting to provide for early spring—for example, combining a variety of spring bulbs with warm-season grasses that are effective from mid-summer on.

☐ Look for abiding summer combinations.

☐ Consider the subtle colors of ornamental grasses at more than one season in choosing companion plants.

☐ Find striking fall combinations.

☐ Let grasses carry on the show after other herbaceous plants have turned to dry sticks.

☐ Enjoy grasses' winter presence, and plan for contrast among them and with conifers and broadleaf evergreens.

☐ Use grasses in a naturalistic garden as a logical and fitting corollary to the way grasses grow in nature.

5. A FEW GOOD COMBINATIONS

F AR FROM BEING subjects to be grouped together in special beds, grasses have just the right qualities to complement the bulbs, perennials, shrubs, and evergreens already growing in our gardens. They work well in just about any garden situation, but there are some particularly brilliant partnerships. The following are tried and true. As more and more grasses are grown in our gardens, hundreds of new combinations will be tried.

HAPPY MARRIAGES

These are exceptionally enduring combinations that maintain their attractive relationship even as the plants change dramatically from one season to the next.

Fountain grass (*Pennisetum alopecuroides*) and black-eyed Susan (*Rudbeckia fulgida* 'Goldsturm')

This is a combination that has been made famous by the landscape architectural firm of Oehme, van Sweden & Associates, Inc. They created stylized "city meadows" using large numbers of both of these plants in adjacent masses. Crucial to the success of this combination is the fact that both plants grow to the same height. The cultivar 'Goldsturm' of the many forms of black-eyed Susan

ABOVE: Porcupine grass rises above a low-growing ground cover of (from left to right) plumbago, yellow-blooming *Coreopsis verticillata,* and mugo pine. (Brookside Gardens)

(*Rudbeckia*) can be counted upon to do this. Both 'Goldsturm' and fountain grass bloom in July, and both remain showy for a very long period. A stylized meadow of these two plants is a delight to look upon in the summer. After more than a month of summer bloom, the meadow continues to be attractive throughout fall. The two plants fade into winter via the subtle colors of fall. It is in winter, however, that the absolute genius of this combination is evident. Fountain grass turns bright almond color and hangs onto its seeds into winter, while black-eyed Susan's flowers become deep, chocolate brown balls of seeds. Together they compose another long and spectacular season of show.

Fountain grass (*Pennisetum alopecuroides*) and white hydrangeas (*Hydrangea paniculata grandiflora*)

Fountain grass and P.G. hydrangeas are an extremely subtle but nonetheless memorable combination whose grand alliance is based upon the simultaneous appearance of creamy white flowers on both plants that last for a month in late summer. At a time when other plants show signs of heat exhaustion and general weariness, fountain grass and P.G. hydrangeas combine as a fresh, cool, green and creamy white focus. At the edge of a lawn or along the margin of a property, the mingling of their flowers is reason enough to grow this gentle combination. What happens in fall, however, is an added incentive: The flowers of both plants age in unison, with fountain grass turning the color of old lace tinged with pink and the big balls of hydrangea flowers being brushed pink by the sun.

The presence of other ornamental grasses or perennials with pink to red coloring augments the picture. The following plants are superb fall companions: the soft purple-pink coneflowers (*Echinacea purpurea*), pinkish tan fountain grass, pink-blushing P.G. hydrangea, *Sedum* 'Autumn Joy' (turning throughout fall from a soft to a deep rose), a clump or two of bright red Japanese blood grass, and the silky rose-colored fans of Eulalia grass.

Spodiopogon sibiricus and day lilies

Spodiopogon makes an excellent specimen, needing so much room to develop that it is at its best with very little competition. A mature clump of spodiopogon may open out to six feet wide at bloom time. It is most attractive without any tall plants nearby to confine its graceful spread. Because it will tolerate light shade and is not showy after frost, it is ideally grown in a large bed of low ground cover. Japanese irises and the low-growing day lilies accent spodiopogon wonderfully. Both provide summer color but are low enough not to detract from this grass's distinctive habit.

At the Gratz garden in Baltimore, snowy white hydrangeas bloom in concert with fountain grass (*Pennisetum alopecuroides*, in the foreground). At left is *Spodiopogon sibiricus* and at right a miscanthus. A river of black-eyed Susans winds through the planting. (Design: Wolfgang Oehme)

Tall grasses *Arundo donax* and *Miscanthus sinensis* grow in concert with the 'Cherokee Chief' sedum, which is lettuce green all summer long, and shows spectacular color in fall. Inflorescences in the foreground belong to *Calamagrostis arundinacea brachytricha*.

61

Evergreen ground covers like myrtle (*Vinca minor*), pachysandra, or ivy are a consideration because, after frost, spodiopogon turns a dull brown. At that point, cut it back and allow the bed of ground cover to provide form and interest throughout the winter.

COLOR COORDINATION

Teaming colored grasses with similarly colored and sympathetic companions heightens their effect in the garden.

Porcupine grass (*Miscanthus sinensis strictus*) and yellow flowers and foliage

All by itself, porcupine grass is a riveting specimen. More erect and upright in habit than zebra grass, it has the same striking coloring, with light green foliage banded horizontally in yellow. The yellow bands of porcupine grass are even more prominent when rising out of a field of the lower-growing yellow yarrows or of other yellow plants—for example, *Coreopsis verticillata*.

Yarrows to be grown with porcupine grass have to be chosen with care. The big ones like 'Coronation Gold' are much too big and will swiftly engulf the grass, although they might serve as a backdrop. *Achillea tomentosa* or the variety 'Moonshine' are good choices because they are short enough not to overwhelm the porcupine grass or need staking. The glaucous green of the yarrow foliage and the light green of the porcupine grass are pleasing together and an excellent foil for the bright golden yellow of both flowers and bands.

Another excellent companion to porcupine grass is the *Hosta* 'August Moon.' Its rippled, cleanly cut, rounded leaves are a beautiful foil to the long slender blades of the grass. Its solid greenish yellow color is a perfect match to the variegated bands of the grass. And its low growth—only about one foot high—sets off the grass's upright vase shape.

White and green variegated grasses—*Miscanthus sinensis variegata, Phalaris arundinacea picta*—with variegated plants and pastels

Longitudinally green and white striped Eulalia grass (*Miscanthus sinensis variegata*) grows slightly less tall than the species and tolerates light shade. Some say its color is brighter and clearer in this situation. With other variegated plants, it forms soothing combinations for the hot days of summer that will work far into fall.

Ribbon grass, or gardener's garters (*Phalaris arundinacea picta*), is a robustly rhizomatous green and white grass that is undemanding in its cultural requirements. It quickly forms lively, fresh-looking ground cover that is truly trouble-free.

The white variegation of these grasses always adds a cool note to a planting. It also brings life to the garden. The flash of white makes it appear that something is happening in the garden when nothing is blooming.

When the white and green colors are very nearly equal, as they are in the striped Eulalia and the ribbon grass, the effect is of a soft pastel green that softens an otherwise all-encompassing green and makes the garden a more welcome and fitting place for the delicate pastels of roses. The silver-edged dogwood (*Cornus alba argenteo-marginata*), with white-edged leaves, has the same effect and serves as an ideal background plant for striped Eulalia or ribbon grass in a pastel color scheme.

Mainly deep green plants like the white-edged plantain lily (*Hosta undulata* 'Albo-marginata' or *Hosta decorata* 'Thomas Hogg') are interesting companions of the striped Eulalia because their spare variegation—a thin white edge—contrasts with and highlights the white of the grass.

Blue-gray grasses and the new variegated *Miscanthus sinensis* 'Morning Light'

Any one of the small "blue" grasses serves admirably in a garden of white and glaucous gray-green colored plants. Dusty Miller, artemesias, lamb's ears, lavender, santolina, and *Perovskia* work well with blue grasses. Nurseryman Kurt Bluemel likes to add the new miscanthus *M. sinensis* 'Morning Light' to the gray-blue garden because its variegated foliage is so fine it has an almost glaucous appearance. One good blue fescue is the *Festuca ovina* 'Harz,' a very early and heavy bloomer. Lacy ice blue-green flowers appear right after tulips bloom. Flowers are carried on hundreds of long, thin stems. They effectively treble the size and impact of the plant, appearing while and after Oriental poppies bloom, but before lavender and rose campion (*Lychnis coronaria*). Later the seeds will turn a pale tan color. Where the change in the compact, neat hummock shape of the fescue to a broad, blooming vase shape is not desirable, another fescue that usually does not bloom, 'Solling,' can be substituted. Other fescues for the gray garden include blue sheep's fescue (*Festuca ovina* 'Superba'), which grows about eight inches tall and is a cool, silvery blue and *Festuca* 'Limerock 15,' only six inches tall and a clean, pure blue.

Lyme grass (*Elymus*) or blue oat grass (*Helictotrichon sempervirens*) and gray plants

Gertrude Jekyll, the illustrious English garden designer, used native English blue lyme grass in her gray garden border, surrounding it with soapwort, lavender, nepeta, sea kale, and santolina against a backdrop of tamarisk. In her book *Colour Schemes for the Flower Garden*, she wrote: "Further back [behind the blue foliage of sea kale] is the fine blue foliage of Lyme-grass *(Elymus arenarius)*, a plant of our sea-shores, but of much value for blue effects in the garden." Pictured in Miss Jekyll's book is the combination of lyme grass and santolina. The American native lyme grass *(Elymus glaucus)* with its sharp, clean blue-gray is the bluest of all the grasses.

Because lyme grass is notoriously invasive, an easier-to-handle blue grass with a more distinct hedgehog-like habit and finer blades is blue oat grass *(Helictotrichon sempervirens)*. Blue oat grass is a two-foot mound of spikey, blue, narrow blades that blooms in May. Flowers appear first on long, arching stems that turn yellow-tan and persist for months, bobbing over the plants and dancing in the wind. Another good companion for either lyme or oat grass is *Koeleria argentea,* a ten-inch bright silver-gray grass that flowers white at the time lavender comes into bud and throughout its bloom. Lacy flowers later deepen to almond. Seeds are light tan, long, and narrow.

Blue sheep's fescue *(Festuca amethystina* 'Superba'), lamb's ear *(Stachys byzantina)*, and creeping juniper

This combination makes an excellent informal edging for a white garden or along a terrace or path where its "white" color is particularly effective at night. All three are low—fescue only eight inches tall, the lamb's ear perhaps half of that, and the juniper, depending upon species, anywhere from two inches to one foot tall. Together they do a good job of framing taller, leggier plants. They are an excellent foreground for the early blue-flowering plants: Dutch iris, cat mint, and blue flax. Their different habits—the lamb's ear, ground hugging and irregular in growth; the fescue, erect, regular, and globose; and the juniper, textured and horizontal—create a pleasant contrast.

While their shapes contrast, their colors are a perfect blend. The color of the blades and stems of the fescue is exactly that of the lamb's ear underneath its fuzzy white coating. The flower color of the fescue approximates the mix of the lamb's ear's undercolor and fuzzy outer coating, and blends with the juniper's deeper blue-green. In hot climates, the fescue may brown out during the hottest months, but the lamb's ear and juniper, unscathed by heat and drought, will carry on until the fescue revives.

Flame grass *(Miscanthus sinensis purpurascens),* low green ground cover, and evergreens

All summer long, flame grass is a quietly green, rather upright clump of about three feet of foliage with no hint of its fall flamboyance. As summer wanes, it sends up silky magenta flower fans, and its broad blades turn to bright orange-red in concert and combination with the dogwoods. After frost, although the color fades a bit, it is visible far into winter. In both fall and winter, flame grass looks most striking when contrasted with dark green.

Flame grass is outstanding rising out of low mounding ground cover like the threadleaf coreopsis (*Coreopsis verticillata* 'Moonbeam'), which, while not evergreen, has an almost evergreen effect. All summer its light yellow flowers appear by the hundreds on dark green, airy one-foot mounds of fine threadlike foliage. As fall advances, the mounds darken to a dark gray-green, a fantastic foil for the autumn color of the flame grass. In winter, the coreopsis is a matte thundercloud gray, while the flame grass fades to a pale pumpkin color.

Flame grass is also effective rising out of evergreen ground covers such as low-growing, sun-loving junipers, red-berried cotoneaster, or candytuft (*Iberis sempervirens).* When sited against large hollies ('Nellie R. Stevens,' 'Fosteri,' 'Burfordii'), its late red color picks up the color of berries and contrasts with dark, shiny green leaves.

ATTRACTIVE OPPOSITES

Grasses are nothing if not soft. In the following combinations their amorphous forms contrast with cleanly defined or angular companions.

Giant allium *(Allium giganteum)* and fountain grass *(Pennisetum alopecuroides)*

The brilliant combination of giant allium and fountain grass is absolutely superb in June when the alliums bloom. Their great, long-lasting purple globes—fully six inches in diameter—are held about a foot above the soft, full mounds of the fountain grass. The rosettes of foliage at the base of the alliums are completely hidden by the grass, making the appearance of the flowers a delightful and unexpected surprise. After two weeks of vibrant purple, allium blooms begin to fade to an attractive silvery gray.

Grasses and roses

This is a combination that has been popular in Germany for years. Grass provides the softness, the filler, and the form lacking in the rose bush. And the rose bush provides the rose. Designer

The soft fullness of grasses combines well with angular, colorful scented roses. Switch grass *(Panicum virgatum)* combines with fields of roses at Brookside Gardens in Wheaton, Maryland. (Brookside Gardens)

Benedikt Wasmuth likes 'White Iceberg' with pennisetum. Switch grass *(Panicum virgatum)* is another good voluminous grass partner to roses.

GRASSES IN ROCK GARDENS

Grasses and rocks are handsome partners. In rock gardens, curious seeds and small vibrant grasses invite close inspection.

Mosquito grass *(Bouteloua gracilis)*

Mosquito grass is a prairie grass that carries wonderful, hairy seeds held horizontally on rather stiff upright fine stems above a foot-tall mound of fine foliage. The grass's name is said to derive from the resemblance of the seed heads to mosquito larvae. It could as well be called "minnow grass" because, held as they are at different heights above the mound, the seeds look like fish swimming in all directions at different depths. Mosquito grass is drought-tolerant.

Bearskin grass *(Festuca scoparia)*

Bearskin grass is a beautiful addition to a rock garden, if only for its brilliant emerald green color. It grows only about six inches tall but, if given room enough, will eventually spread to a yard in diameter. In June, delicate golden tan flowers are held about a foot above the plant.

Velvet grass *(Holcus lanatus variegatus)*

Velvet grass is a cool-season grass—at its absolute best in the early spring when bulbs bloom. A bright, stunning white with narrow green stripes, it is a densely tufted, mat-forming velvety carpet that grows to about eight inches tall. It requires sandy soil and dislikes hot, humid climates, where it tends to brown out by mid-summer. Even with this disadvantage, velvet grass brings so much to the early spring garden that it is worth growing anywhere.

Japanese blood grass (*Imperata cylindrica* 'Red Baron')

Small—only eighteen inches tall—and delicate, stunning green and red blood grass needs a place in the foreground of a planting where it can be seen and appreciated. A single plant isn't enough to make a statement. Blood grass looks good in groups of three or small fields of a dozen or more. A position where the rising or setting sun will backlight the grass is best.

Green and red Japanese blood grass (*Imperata Cylindrica* 'Red Baron') and striking black mondo grass (*Ophiopogon planiscapus* 'Ebony Knight') flank a stone pathway at the Brookside Botanic Gardens.

GRASSES FOR PONDS OR POOLS

Nothing suits a garden pool or a pond as well as ornamental grasses. Their gracefully pendant habits—like fountains caught in the act of spewing water—perfectly complement an aquatic setting. Many grasses suit this situation.

Maiden grass (*Miscanthus sinensis* 'Gracillimus')

Maiden grass is one of the best at poolside. A five-foot clump of slender, white-veined, gracefully arching blades that grows thicker and more dense with each passing year, maiden grass is both delicate and imposing.

Fountain grass (*Pennisetum alopecuroides*)

Shorter and broader than maiden grass, fountain grass (*Pennisetum alopecuroides*), which grows about thirty inches tall and spreads three feet, is an ideal companion. Both grasses are similar in habit before bloom, suggesting mature and immature forms of a single species. Planted on one side of a swimming pool, a group of maiden and fountain grasses grants utter privacy. Their dense, lush foliage works at eye level, screening exactly where needed without shading the pool or dropping leaves into it. Grasses also soften the effect of expanses of concrete. When they are well grown, which takes about three years, they shelter the pool like a dense, mysterious jungle, and swimmers can have a sense of floating down the Amazon in their own swimming pools.

Common reed (*Phragmites*)

Where it is not already growing, the native common reed (*Phragmites*) is a natural for a pond planting. At home in saturated soil on the margin of a pond, it serves as a good-looking companion to large grasses like those of the miscanthus species. Where it is already growing, large ornamental grasses serve to make the transition from garden to the background of native reed.

The mellics (*Melica transylvanica* and *Melica ciliata*)

Around small garden ponds, smaller grasses accent without overwhelming. Two good ones with just the right cascading habit are the mellics—M. *transylvanica*, almost three feet tall when in bloom, and the smaller M. *ciliata*, only slightly over a foot tall. Both are early (May) bloomers and remain showy for at least two months. Instead of very large miscanthus species as a background, medium-size feather reed grass (*Calamagrostis acutiflora stricta*) or the northern sea oats (*Chasmanthium latifolium*) are better choices.

Graceful maiden grass (*Miscanthus sinensis* 'Gracillimus'), backed by the glaucous native *Phragmites* reed, grows on a pond's edge in designer Jack Lenor Larsen's Long Island garden. (Design: Jack Lenor Larsen)

GRASSES AS TRANSITION TO MEADOW OR WOODLAND

A number of grasses work brilliantly as transition plants, softening an otherwise abrupt edge.

Fountain grass (*Pennisetum alopecuroides*)

Designer Sunny Scully favors edging an uncut meadow adjacent to a lawn with fountain grass to form a graceful transition between the cut and uncut.

Bottle brush grass (*Hystrix patula*) and *Deschampsia caespitosa*

Another place where grasses form a bridge between one kind of vegetation and another is where lawn or pavement meets woodland. Grasses like *Hystrix patula* or *Deschampsia caespitosa*, which originate in this situation in nature, are ideal.

A vigorous, running miscanthus (possibly *M. sacchariflorus*) competes with brambles and perennial weeds and serves as transition between the edge of woodland and this large country garden. Root competition and shade contain growth on the woodland side, and mowing and pulling up stray plants on the garden side keep the grass within bounds. Day lilies are tough enough to hold their own.

GIANT GRASSES AND BOLD PERENNIALS

Giant grasses like Eulalia grass, maiden grass, giant miscanthus, and giant reed need fitting companion plants. Bold, large-scale perennials—often those that are too large and coarse-looking for ordinary garden situations—work beautifully with the big grasses. Some to consider are boltonias, cow parsnips, and Joe Pye weed. Their foliage provides contrasting form and texture while their flowers add color.

Mixing bold perennials with equally bold grasses creates dramatic tableaux. Cunningly sited, these bold groups transform the flattest rectangles, the most inauspicious backyards, into gardens of great mystery. The heights and volumes of imposing grasses and companion perennials work to alter radically our perceptions of space in the garden. Used in the background, large plants blur boundaries and suggest infinite garden. Placed in the foreground, they force perspective and increase apparent depth. Next to a path, they create a passage through the garden that is rife with adventure. Unlike hedges, groups of grasses and perennials do not form walls but create spot screens that conceal only partially. This partial concealment both entices the eye and suggests secret spaces in the depth of garden beyond.

Boltonia asteroides

Flowering white in late summer and fall, *Boltonia* surrounds tall grasses like *Arundo donax* or giant miscanthus (*M. floridulus*) with airy three- to five-foot mounds, covered with white aster-like flowers. The combination of billowing, flowering perennial and upright grass presents a wonderful contrast of form and foliage. Giant miscanthus often becomes leggy below the knees. Flowering *Boltonia* is a beautiful solution to this problem. There is a pink form, *Boltonia asteroides* 'Pink Beauty.'

Cardoon (Cynara cardunculus)

Cardoon, an imposing leviathan with striking gray-green foliage, grows to six feet tall. It is brightly tomentose on the undersides of colossal spine-tipped leaves. As befits a relative of the globe artichoke, cardoon's thickened leaf stalks and roots are edible. Give cardoon plenty of room to develop.

Massive, glaucous cardoon *(Cynara cardunculus)* and blue lyme grass *(Elymus)* combine in artist Bob Dash's Long Island garden. (Design: Bob Dash)

Eupatorium towers above giant grasses—variegated giant reed *(Arundo donax variegata)* and *Miscanthus sinensis* 'Gracillimus'—at the North Carolina State Botanic Garden. (Design: Edith Eddleman)

Joe Pye weed *(Eupatorium purpureum)*

Joe Pye weed is another tall, bold North American native that blooms purple in very late summer. It, too, works well punctuating a field of homogenous grasses and forbs. It could be planted among switch grasses *(Panicum virgatum)* or fountain grasses *(Pennisetum alopecuroides)*, alongside of giant miscanthus, or as a background plant for maiden and Eulalia grass.

Jerusalem artichoke *(Helianthus tuberosus)*

Also edible, yellow-flowering Jerusalem artichoke, which grows to ten feet tall, is a good and practical companion to large grasses. Its habit is extremely upright and thin.

Cow parsnip *(Heracleum mantegazzianum)*

Neither the common nor the botanical name of the cow parsnip *(Heracleum mantegazzianum)* is melodic, but both are fitting. With seven feet of spindly stems supporting huge, coarse, toothed two-foot leaves, the cow parsnip is a plant impossible to ignore. Yet for all of its size, it doesn't block but merely channels our line of vision. It is a good companion to *Miscanthus sinensis*, over which it will tower but—lacking the grass's volume—will not dominate. Someday, perhaps someone with lots of room and a taste for the dramatic will plant a giant's meadow of tall grasses punctuated by cow parsnips.

Plume poppy *(Macleaya cordata)*

Like the big grasses, plume poppy can astound us with its prodigious growth. A perennial, hardy to Zone 3, plume poppy shoots up seven- to eight-foot stalks that bear long, lacy plumes of tan coral in early summer. Plume poppies, by virtue of aggressively spreading suckers, form dense groups.

Tartarian aster *(Aster tataricus)*

Tartarian aster grows up to six feet, spreading by rhizomes into tall, dark green colonies topped by feathery lavender-blue. Flowers are borne at the top of very upright, unbranched stems that give the plant a distinctly narrow, vertical character, a contrast to broad grasses like *Miscanthus sinensis* and cultivars.

ABOVE: Maiden grass and rose mallows used as a screen (Brookside Gardens)

6. GRASSES FOR SPECIALIZED GARDEN USE

TODAY'S GARDENS TEND toward freer forms and a somewhat more naturalistic overall impression. Even so, there is invariably a plan to any garden. It isn't just a random grouping of plants. The final effect may appear carefree and spontaneous, but, chances are, it is the end result of calculated arrangement. Before a plant can be carefully positioned for the desired impact, a gardener must take into account its cultural needs and growth patterns and determine whether its particular ornamental traits are compatible with his or her overall design scheme.

Fortunately, ornamental grasses include a rich diversity of species and cultivars that lend themselves to different uses and places in the garden. And quite a few perform brilliantly in outdoor living spaces as container plants or indoors as material for bouquets and arrangements. This chapter notes the best grasses for specialized garden use.

COLOR YOU CAN COUNT ON

Because ornamental grasses are foliage plants, we can depend upon their blues, rusts, reds, yellows, and variegations throughout the summer. Dependable color is a great boon anywhere, but in climates where summers are hot and the show of perennials is often disappointingly short-lived, it is truly a friend in need. If we cannot

74

count on perennials for enduring color, we can grow colorful grasses. They are season-long sources of reliable color, against which perennials play off in transient augmentation and accent.

In addition to other colors, there is a vast range of greens among their number—from the bright yellow-green of *Milium* to the dark leathery straplike foliage of *Carex* and *Deschampsia.* Later on in the fall, most ornamental grasses turn fleetingly and fittingly to gold, rust, apricot, and brown, while a few produce spectacular hues. Finally, a good number of grasses have outstanding winter color, remaining gold and wheat or almond and taupe throughout the winter. Any one of these colorful grasses can serve as a constant in the garden's color scheme.

Large grasses, whatever their color, are prepossessing in a border. When they are colored blue-green or red or yellow, they are too distinctive for any sort of secondary role. Their size and foliage distinguish them as the plants that give structure and define the color scheme of the garden. They have to be considered first, and other plants—more fleeting and more subtle—have to be situated in relation to them.

The Greens

We are so accustomed to green in the landscape that we tend not to count it as a color. Close attention to greens, however, can result in a finely tuned planting in which the hue and intensity of the component greens can make plants blend or contrast, advance or recede. For example, the bright yellow-green of *Sesleria autumnalis* rushes forward to meet the eye, while the soft, pale green-dusted blue of *Arundo donax* seems to recede. The deep, rich greens found in *Deschampsia caespitosa, Ophiopogon japonicus* 'Kyoto,' and the emerald-colored bearskin fescue (*Festuca scoparia*) contrast with and stand apart from most other greens. The entire genus *Miscanthus* can be counted upon for winter color. Among their number, the giant grasses—Eulalia grass (*Miscanthus sinensis*) and maiden grass (*M. sinensis* 'Gracillimus')—have two seasons of distinctly different color. In summer, they are a voluminous and undulating green, a cool, clean foil for the hot colors of perennial flowers. In fall, green bleeds gradually to a dull pastel. After repeated frosts, grasses blanch almond and, brittle and bright, contrast smartly with evergreens.

Many greens, of course, slip easily into that great blanketing, neutral garden-of-Eden green found everywhere—in lawns, on the tops of trees, and in summer hedges. This neutral sort of green is enormously valuable in the garden, where it functions diplomatically, mediating between colors that might otherwise overwhelm or clash. The light and medium greens of fountain grass

(*Pennisetum alopecuroides*) and maiden grass (*Miscanthus sinensis* 'Gracillimus') separate and frame brilliant oranges, fuchsias, purple, and blues of summer flowers. Yet these same neutral shades are surprisingly bright when planted beside dark hollies and yews.

The Blues

"Blue" grasses range from the very slightest tinge of blue in the foliage of pampas grass to the giant reed (*Arundo donax*), a soft, dusty, pale green with a slight blue cast, to the brilliant ice blue-gray of the blue fescue (*Festuca cinerea superba*). In between are dozens of others, the largest group of which are found in the genus *Festuca*, which contains more than a hundred species of annual and perennial grasses. The blue fescue most readily available is commonly labeled *Festuca ovina*, *Festuca ovina glauca*, or sometimes *Festuca glauca*. It is a blue-green hummock of eight-inch slender blades that makes a fine ground cover in sun. Gardeners may pick and choose among many cultivars of gray-blue fescues. Other blues besides the giant reed and the fescues include *Koeleria*, *Helictotrichon*, *Carex nigra*, and *Elymus*.

Variegated Grasses

Variegated ornamental grasses are some of the hardest-working subjects in the garden. Their constant color often functions as a brightener for dull spots in the landscape. Variegated grasses are a source of permanent, reliable color in the garden against which other plants can be played off as they come into their period of bloom. Variegated grasses may be pure white and green like the Japanese silver sedge (*Carex morrowii variegata*) or ribbon grass (*Phalaris arundinacea picta*) or variegated miscanthus (*M. sinensis variegatus*). They may be a combination of cream and green like variegated liriope or the variegated Japanese sedge (*Carex morrowii aureo-variegata*). When the variegation is of white and green, the effect is particularly suited to pastels and clear reds and blues. A combination of very pale, delicately colored flowers—such as pink roses with variegated dogwood—and ribbon grass is always well balanced. Tender hues are not overwhelmed but enhanced by green and white variegation, which tends to make the whole color scheme more delicate.

Cream to yellow-colored variegation works better with deep greens and warm colors in the gold to orange range. The variegated *Arundinaria* (bamboo) and variegated liriope work especially well with deep greens.

Golden and Yellow Grasses

Golden grasses add the glow of sunlight to the garden. Bowles Golden grass (*Carex stricta* 'Bowles Golden'), bright yellow-green golden grass *(Milium effusum aureum),* and yellow foxtail grass *(Alopecurus praetensis aureus)* splash the garden with their sunny foliage. Porcupine grass *(Miscanthus sinensis strictus)* is a green grass with horizontal yellow bands.

Red and Purple Grasses

With the exception of the red forms of *Pennisetum setaceum,* which are hardy only to Zone 8, Japanese blood grass *(Imperata cylindrica* 'Red Baron') is the only perennial grass that is red throughout the season. Although the base of each leaf blade begins as a bright green, the rest of the blade turns a brilliant blood red. Each color is heightened by the other. Japanese blood grass grows about eighteen inches tall and spreads slowly by rhizomes and is more vivid with three or more hours of direct sun each day. It is not invasive.

Pennisetum setaceum rubrum, a deep wine red, and *P. setaceum atropurpureum,* a purple-red, are treated as annuals in most parts of the country. Both are outstanding sources of season-long color. They are hardy in Zone 8.

Black and Brown Grasses

Black mondo grass (*Ophiopogon japonicus* 'Ebony Knight') is closest to black. Not a true grass, black mondo grass grows to about six inches of purple-black foliage that is most effective when contrasted with yellow or bright green or with Japanese blood grass.

New Zealand sedge *(Carex buchananii),* an army drab/cinnamon brown, isn't the easiest plant to place because of its unusual color. It needs companion plants that do not overwhelm its soft color, or plants that contrast with it. Deep green foliage and yellow and cream-colored flowers are lively companions.

Fall Colors

In addition to their spring and summer foliage colors, many grasses reward us with a second season of show by turning colors in the fall. Perhaps the most spectacular of these is flame grass *(Miscanthus sinensis purpurascens).* All summer long, flame grass stays a clear, bright, medium green. It is a good filler, a quietly handsome subject that produces lovely, silken magenta plumes in late summer. Then, just as the tree leaves turn, flame grass undergoes a meta-

Slightly larger than the New Zealand sedge *(Carex buchananii)* C. *flagelifera*, a light brown—orange sedge (center), grows in a San Francisco garden flanked by phormiums, agave, and succulents. (Photo by John Greenlee)

Olive drab *Carex buchananii* is surrounded by color-coordinated companions in designer Edith Eddleman's North Carolina garden.

morphosis. Suddenly, it is a show-stopper, an impossible-to-over-look, riveting bright orange-red with dazzling white flowers. When it is viewed with light streaming through the foliage, the effect is truly that of a brilliant fire in the garden. The very best position for flame grass is one where it can be viewed from two sides at different times of day, with both the rising and setting sun backlighting it. After frost, the color fades a bit, but is still attractive and remains so throughout the winter.

Prairie cord grass (*Spartina pectinata aureo-marginata*) is another fall dazzler. Matte medium-green, sometimes with fine yellow stripes along the margins of its cascading blades, prairie cord grass turns a clear bright yellow in the fall.

Red switch grass (*Panicum virgatum* 'Rotstrahlbusch') grows only three feet tall and bears clouds of red seeds above the plants in late summer. The entire grass colors red in the fall. Other cultivars of red switch grass are 'Rehbraun' and 'Haense Herms.'

Many other ornamental grasses turn shades of apricot and orange, too, but they do so fleetingly. Among these are palm sedge (*Carex muskingumensis*), giant miscanthus (*M. floridulus*), and fountain grass (*Pennisetum alopecuroides*). We can enjoy their autumn show for only a few days before they begin to fade into winter.

Even when the fall colors of ornamental grasses are not brilliant, they are always seasonally appropriate. Grasses take part in a gradual, global transformation from high summer with its lush greens and brilliant flower colors to the subtle, earth-toned palette of autumn. As they turn, unlike many perennials, which lose volume as they dry, grasses hold their shape. This allows them to grow old gracefully and also to bestow grace upon the garden in which they grow. Their continued fullness softens the angularity of dried stalks and stems. The whole garden takes on the soft, subtle hues of a country field in autumn.

Winter Color

No other garden subjects are so highly regarded in their dormant state as are the ornamental grasses. Of what other group of plants can it be said that we eagerly anticipate their performance, their color, their effectiveness in the garden in winter, when the plants are dead? Some gardeners regard grasses like switch grass (*Panicum virgatum*) and fountain grass (*Pennisetum alopecuroides*) as at their absolute best and most showy in the dead of winter, when they have been blanched to shades of wheat and almond by repeated frosts.

Winter-colored grasses blow in a cold January wind at the International Center Park in Washington, D.C. After frost, colors never clash. Here colors of dormant grasses—pumpkin-hued flame grass *(Miscanthus purpurascens)* and almond-hued Eulalia grass *(Miscanthus sinensis)* blend perfectly with the rusty browns of *Hypericum* (foreground) and dried seed heads of *Sedum telephium* 'Autumn Joy' (background). (Design: Oehme, van Sweden & Associates, Inc.)

GRASSES AS GROUND COVERS

Traditionally, ground covers have been low-growing evergreen plants like ivy, pachysandra, or myrtle. They were planted either for eye appeal or to save the labor involved in maintaining a lawn. By expanding the traditional definition of "ground cover," far more exciting and attractive options are possible. Large masses of a single ornamental grass provide ground cover material with the uniform appearance that is suitable for landscaping.

Most grasses are neither short nor evergreen. And this is good. In the words of landscape designer Edith Eddleman, "Gardens need grasses to lift them up and out and above themselves." Taller groups of plants have greater impact on a landscape scale, and herbaceous material is far more exciting and dynamic than evergreen material. In addition, some ornamental grasses have enormous winter presence.

Most ornamental grasses make superb ground covers. The quiet beauty of a single plant is magnified when multiples of one kind of grass are used. Large masses of one kind of grass magnify the dynamics of a single plant: the way it greens up in the spring, its summer fullness, its bloom, its winter coloring. Even the most subtle characteristics are enhanced by repetition. A single *Festuca amethystina* 'Bronzeglanz' bears seeds that are tinted a rosy brown in summer. Where this rather subdued color is not particularly striking on a single specimen, when many plants are grouped together the colored seed heads create a shimmering rainbow effect. Grouped together, other ornamental grasses—the fountain grasses and feather reed grass—endow even a small city lot with the nostalgic beauty of a country field.

Although ornamental grasses range from just a few inches to several feet in height, the taller the grass, the more sound and movement it will bring into the garden. A field of thirty-six-inch fountain grass (*Pennisetum alopecuroides*) or five-foot-tall switch grass (*Panicum virgatum*) is never completely still. The slightest breath of wind will set the arching stems to quivering and whispering. A lively, little breeze playing through a field of grasses streaks its surface with rivers of silver and blue and causes the whole to surge and rush and billow like the sea.

As shimmering and beautiful as grasses are in summer, some people find ornamental grasses at their most appealing during the winter. However, not all grasses are equally decorative after frost. Nor do all grasses go dormant. The list of grasses for use as ground covers that follows has been subdivided to group together characteristics desirable in ground covers. Included are those that have outstanding winter presence, those that are evergreen, those that grow rampantly, those that thrive in the shade, and those that make very early growth in the spring.

Ground Cover Grasses with Outstanding Winter Presence

"Growing old gracefully" is a phrase that applies to several perennial ornamental grasses. All are attractive from the moment they emerge from the ground in spring. All flower gracefully and hold their seed heads for a very long time. All make welcome additions to the summer garden. All are stunning knockouts after frost and far into winter, when their foliage is withered and dry.

Fountain grass (*Pennisetum alopecuroides*)

Fountain grass is the best all-around ground cover choice for a position in full sun to part shade. It is also one of the most economical for ground cover over a large area, because it is possible to grow any number of plants easily from seed. Plants in their first year from seed may flower only sparsely, but they will grow large enough—about eighteen inches—to make an attractive showing. Although they flower profusely the second year, they will not reach their full potential until the third year from seed.

When used as a ground cover, fountain grass should be spaced at twenty-four- to thirty-six-inch intervals, depending upon how quickly coverage and how smooth a surface is wanted. Larger spaces in between leave room for bulbs and create a slightly more hummocky surface. Giant crocuses, daffodils, and tulips are ideal candi-

Fountain grass (*Pennisetum alopecuroides*) covers a slope under a dogwood at Brookside Gardens in Wheaton, Maryland.

dates for spring color. Later on, the large alliums—both the June-blooming giant allium (*A. giganteum*) and the earlier, slightly smaller *A. aflatunense*—are stunning purple globes carried on strong stems above tufts of soft green fountain grass. After the flowers fade, alliums turn to silvery spheres of vibrating seeds.

By mid-May in the mid-Atlantic states, fountain grass is over a foot tall and will quickly attain its full height of about thirty-six inches. The South will be some weeks ahead, while the North will be two to four weeks behind. Individual blades of fountain grass are longer than thirty-six inches, but cascade gracefully, endowing the plant with the habit that inspired its common name and is its great charm.

After frost, fountain grass gradually turns to a bright almond color. At first, blades are streaked with green, but gradually the green fades away. Seed heads persist on the plants into winter until the wind has blown them away. Even with a fair amount of wind damage, fountain grass stays attractive until spring, when it is cut back. In fact, it is a great temptation to put off this task because the plants provide substance at a time when the garden is still quite bare. It is, however, very important to cut fountain grass back each year in early spring (February–March). Otherwise the old, faded blades will mix with new green growth. While each phase has its special charm, mixed together they look dishevelled. If the gardener waits too long to cut back the grasses, he or she will have to cut in and around fresh new growth to remove the old. In addition, there is then the risk of treading on emerging bulbs.

Where lower ground cover is called for, the smaller forms of fountain grass, *Pennisetum alopecuroides* 'Hameln' and the lower-growing 'Weserbergland' (both growing twenty-four to thirty-six inches) are good choices. The more tender (hardy in Zone 7) *P. Orientale*, growing to only twenty-four inches, blooms three weeks earlier than *P. alopecuroides*, with cottony flowers. *P. caudatum*, the white-flowering fountain grass, has a more erect habit and may reach almost five feet in the perfect spot.

Switch grass (*Panicum virgatum*)

The best grass for winter show, switch grass can reach eight feet tall, although three to five feet is more common. For some people, even three feet may be stretching the definition of ground cover entirely too far. In summer, switch grass is a dusty soft green that is crowned by lacy flowers in late June. One often sees it bowed under the weight of its flowers and pliant, long stems. Depending upon the viewer, this characteristic may be described either as "elegantly languid" or "floppy." Planted in a mass, plants tend to hold each other up. When seeds develop, they form a glistening, cloudlike layer over the plants.

In winter, frost turns switch grass a wheat color and stiffens its blades. It stands erect and, when planted in a mass, creates a remarkably even, uniform block of golden plants.

Divide plants in spring before they have begun their active growth. Lift clumps and shake off the soil to pull the roots apart gently. Because it doesn't begin active growth until mid-spring, interplant switch grass with daffodils, tulips, early alliums, or Oriental poppies, all of whose foliage disappears by mid-summer. Unlike clump-forming fountain grass, switch grass spreads to eventually fill in between plants, ultimately crowding other plants out. Switch grass is a strong grower and can tolerate some shade, especially in the South and upper South. It is also a good competitor, holding its own against weeds and other grasses.

Red switch grass (*Panicum virgatum* 'Haense Herms,' *P.v.* 'Rotstrahlbusch,' *P.v.* 'Rehbraun')

Red switch grass is lower-growing than switch grass, reaching only about two or three feet. In fall, foliage turns red and red seed clouds hover over the plants. Red switch grass, by virtue of its smaller stature, is somewhat more erect than switch grass. It is an excellent choice for places where the larger form would be overpowering.

Feather reed grass (*Calamagrostis acutiflora stricta*)

Feather reed grass is a strong-growing, medium to dark green grass that is one of the first to revive in spring. When fountain grass is still a clump of dry sticks that is just beginning to show green and switch grass is still dormant, feather reed grass, a cool-season grass, will show almost a foot of strong new growth, pushing headlong up out of the ground to its eventual height of five feet. Because of its unique habit, bearing strongly upright flowers and seeds with a loose collar of branching leaves, clumps of feather reed grass take a long time to blend together into a uniform field.

Feather reed grass has an amazingly long period of show. Not only is it the first to leaf out in spring, its flowers appear in June. They are followed by bright gold seeds held erectly over dense, deep green plants with which they contrast stunningly. A field of these is breathtaking in summer and fall sunshine. In winter, their appearance is even more striking when they become a dazzling bicolored cream and gold.

Feather reed grass makes good strong growth and, if allowed four to five feet between plants, will grow broad. Closer spacing results in more upright growth. This grass will tolerate light shade, but holds its flowers and seeds more erectly when grown in full sun.

Early Ground Cover Grasses

Cool-season grasses resume growth in late winter. By the time the gardener is ready to venture outside again, they are completely revived and in top form, adding color and life to an otherwise bare landscape.

Yellow foxtail grass (*Alopecurus pratensis aureus*)

Yellow foxtail grass is at its best planted in masses where the fine yellow striping on its quarter-inch-wide, flat blades glows yellow-gold in the landscape. The slowly rhizomatous clumps grow about a foot high, flowering in April. Yellow foxtail grass is a cool-season grass, reviving early in the year and adding bright color to the spring landscape. Not surprisingly, yellow foxtail grass is not always at its best in hot weather. In a hot, dry spot, it will die back a bit and lose some of its vibrant color. Keep it moist in hot climates. Yellow foxtail grass provides very good color for the cool seasons in the South and for summer in cool summer areas.

Fescue *(Festuca)*

Fescues come in a variety of silver blues and greens and range in size from the two-foot-tall giant fescue *(Festuca mairei)* to the tiny dwarf bearskin fescue *(Festuca scoparia* 'Pic Carlit'), only three inches tall. All prefer a position in sun and revive early in the spring. A field of fescues never really loses its bumpy, tuftlike texture. Over time, however, a planting in poor soil will look neater and more uniform than one that has been pampered. In soil that is too fertile, fescues can become overgrown and unkempt.

Unlike many other cool-season grasses, most fescues bloom early—in mid- to late spring. Their loose, drooping, lacy flowers are held high above the plants on stems that are taller than the clump. The contrast between the relatively small, round, stiff, immobile plant and its tall, thin, gracefully arching, and gently swaying flower stalks is charming. Cut off flower stalks when they are no longer attractive. In addition to use as ground cover, fescues are ideally suited for the rock garden.

In hot climates, pair fescues with heat-loving plants for an attractive foil during the fescues' off season. 'Solling' usually doesn't flower and never flowers heavily. Not having expended the energy, it remains presentable throughout summer in hot summer areas. Because it doesn't require shearing, it is a good choice for low-maintenance gardens.

The following are some few of the very many attractive cultivars of fescue. They are listed in order of bloom time.

*Harz blue fescue (Festuca cinerea 'Harz')

This "blue" fescue grows about eight inches tall in a tuft of fine, glaucous foliage that has something of an olive green cast to it. In mid-spring, its light gray-green flowers are held about a foot above the plants.

*April Green fescue (Festuca cinerea 'April Gruen')

A group of six-inch-tall April Green fescue is unforgettable in bloom because the flowers are brushed with an unusual and attractive taupe. This cloudy iridescent hue is most apparent at a distance. When one approaches, it seems to fade from plants close at hand and tantalizingly appear on those farther away. In flower, the plant stands about fourteen inches tall.

*Bronze sheep's fescue (*Festuca amethystina* 'Bronzeglanz')

Bronze sheep's fescue is named for the seed heads which form after it bears flowers in May above eight-inch tufts of foliage. When the flowers appear, they are white, but a bronze color appears and deepens as the seeds mature. In flower, the plant stands seventeen inches tall.

*Bearskin grass (*Festuca scoparia*)

The clear, almost glowing emerald green of bearskin grass is reason enough to grow this ground-hugging, densely tufted, six-inch fescue. Contrasting light golden tan seed stalks arch over the plants from June on. Give bearskin grass sun, moisture, and good drainage. In hot summer climates, bearskin grass does better in partial shade.

Ground Covers for Shade and Half Shade

Many shade-loving grasses and sedges are evergreen, making them superb choices for ground covers. Others add color and texture under trees and on the dark side of buildings.

Variegated Japanese sedge (*Carex morrowii aureo-variegata*) and Japanese silver sedge (*C. morrowii variegata*)

The Japanese sedges bring light to dark, dull spaces in the shady garden. Silver sedge is distinctly white-striped, while the variegated form is cream-colored.

Palm sedge (*Carex muskingumensis*)

Like the spokes of parasols, the whorled blades of palm sedge create delicate, feathery texture in the shade. Palm sedge grows to twenty inches but can be cut back both to freshen the planting or to reduce height. Palm sedge is not evergreen and fades from apricot to a warm buff color in winter.

Bowles Golden grass (*Carex stricta* 'Bowles Golden')

Bowles Golden grass, planted in little groups under tall trees, has the effect of splashes of golden sunlight on the forest floor. It is a true golden yellow grass that grows to twelve inches in shade.

Feathery palm sedge *(Carex mus-kingumensis)* serves as a shade-loving ground cover under trees at the Virginia Avenue Gardens in Washington, D.C. (Design: Oehme, van Sweden & Associates, Inc.)

Bowles Golden grass *(Carex stricta* 'Bowles Golden') glows in the C. S. Thomas garden in England. (Photo by Cynthia Woodyard)

Woodrush *(Luzula)*

The evergreen woodrushes come from the moist woodlands and meadows of Europe and western Siberia. They are a better choice for gardens in the Northeast, Midwest, and Northwest than for the deep South. Early bloomers, they hold their curious, long-stemmed flowers above tufts of broad, straplike leaves. The blades are a soft yellow-green in the center of the tuft, darkening to deep green toward the tips. They are little-known but outstanding ground covers. Refreshing substitutes for ivy and pachysandra, woodrushes are excellent at hiding fallen leaves.

*Hairy woodrush *(Luzula pilosa)*

Growing to about a foot tall, the hairy woodrush is a smooth green, slowly spreading evergreen ground cover for shade. Providing rapid cover in deep, moist soil, the hairy woodrush also persists in dry shade.

*Greater woodrush *(Luzula sylvatica)*

In deep, humusy soil, which it prefers, the greater woodrush can reach fifteen inches. It is an excellent ground cover for a shady, woodland situation, where it will quickly outcompete weeds.

Velvet grass *(Holcus lanatus variegatus)*

Beautiful white, delicately striped green velvet grass is at its freshest and best in late winter and early spring. Growing to eight inches tall, it will spread as long as cool weather prevails.

Robustly Growing Ground Covers

Some grasses are just plain aggressive. Too invasive for ordinary garden situations, these grasses often thrive in difficult sites where others fail.

Ribbon grass *(Phalaris arundinacea picta)*

A good plant for a bad place, ribbon grass (also called gardener's garters) moves too fast in good garden soil, where it makes a sensational showing but has to be rigorously kept in bounds. Hard clay slows it down.

Lyme grass *(Elymus glaucus)*

Beautiful blue lyme grass (also called wild rye) will thrive in anything but standing water. Lyme grass is very aggressive in good garden conditions. Perhaps its best use is as a drought-resistant ground cover or accent in sandy soil.

Running pennisetum (*Pennisetum incomptum,* syn. *P. flaccidum*)

Running pennisetum spreads quickly. In fact, it can be invasive. This is not a plant for the best spot in the garden, but for the kind of place where other plants have trouble growing. There its runaway exuberance will be contained by less than ideal growing conditions. It is aggressive enough to overcome odds and make a good showing.

More erect than fountain grass (*P. alopecuroides*), with longer, thinner blades and seed heads, a stand of *P. incomptum*—especially when its narrow, four- to five-inch-long white flowers appear—has a natural, spontaneous, feathery grace that eludes many clump-forming grasses. Running pennisetum can reach and will tolerate a little shade. In winter, it turns the same bright almond as *P. alopecuroides*.

GRASSES AS HEDGES AND SCREENS

Being outside, surrounded by what is green and growing—in utter privacy—is one of the greatest joys of owning a garden. Ornamental grasses, used by themselves or in combination with shrubs and other grasses, make wonderfully satisfying privacy screens. They are effective from early summer until winter when used alone. Combined with fences or evergreens, ornamental grasses create year-round privacy screens.

Screens of ornamental grasses are dense, lush, and mysterious. When they shoot up in early summer, they change the landscape completely. What was spare and flat becomes lush and voluminous. While traditional hedges provide trim, tidy enclosures, grass hedges are thick, flowing, and a bit unruly. They make us feel as if there is great distance between our garden retreat and the maddening crowd. Instead of just a foot or two of green, there is a jungle, a savannah, a complete and impenetrable wilderness to shield us.

Ornamental grasses grow fast. It is not unreasonable to expect a six-foot-tall, three-foot-wide barrier in about three years when using a grass like Eulalia or maiden grass all by itself. It is also possible to grow a proper hedge of multiples of one type of grass. However, for the most complete privacy, a combination of evergreen hedge material such as holly, euonymus, *Ligustrum*, *Viburnum*, and a big miscanthus will combine to form a screen of great depth precisely where depth is needed: at eye level.

Ornamental grasses require only a yearly cutting back to three or four inches above the ground. Otherwise they are virtually maintenance-free. They don't drop leaves or shade out other plants the way trees do. They don't need clipping the way most hedges do. They do not require pesticides, because they are generally untroubled by pests. Provided they receive their late winter cutting back, their appearance is always neat.

Grasses for Tall Screens

Giant reed (*Arundo donax*)

Planted by itself, *Arundo* will grow quickly into a loose, rather open but eye-stopping clump. Well-grown two-gallon plants put in the ground in April will reach ten feet by October. The giant reed is especially effective when sited against evergreens where its faintly glaucous blue-green stands out.

Giant miscanthus (*Miscanthus floridulus*)

A two-gallon giant miscanthus placed in the ground in April will reach about six or seven feet tall and perhaps two feet in diameter by its first October. After three years, with no special treatment whatsoever, plants placed five feet apart in sun will have very nearly grown together and will be about eight or nine feet tall. Sometimes bare "below the knees," *Miscanthus floridulus* is a perfect backdrop for perennials. Giant miscanthus, like all ornamental grasses, responds to good treatment. If you want a privacy screen in a hurry, coddle your giant miscanthus with compost, manure, fertilizer, sun, and plenty of moisture.

Looking like a green waterfall, giant miscanthus (*Miscanthus floridulus*) screens a private living area. Other grasses—low, variegated ribbon grass (*Phalaris arundinacea picta*, extreme left and right), porcupine grass (*Miscanthus sinensis strictus*, right), and a blooming gray fescue (*Festuca*)—add depth. (Design: Teesh Rehill; photo: Cathy Barash)

Eulalia grass (*Miscanthus sinensis*)

From summer until late in winter, Eulalia grass provides eye-level screening. Shorter than *Miscanthus floridulus,* any one of the varieties of *Miscanthus sinensis* would work well with the giant miscanthus and evergreens, creating deep layers of privacy around an outdoor living area.

Black bamboo (*Phyllostachys nigra*)

Where winter temperatures don't drop below 0°F and where it can be contained, the black bamboo, which grows to twenty-six feet tall, is a glorious screen. Canes come up green but turn black by the end of their first season. Strong sunshine brings out the darkest, deepest color in the culms.

Grasses for Spot Screens

Sometimes planting a whole hedge is overkill. When the problem is not screening an entire outdoor living area for privacy, but blocking out a single unpleasant sight—the neighbors' garbage cans, patio, or driveway—a well-placed giant grass or a grass against a background of shrubs may do the trick. Even if a combination of evergreen and grass is not opaque, it will stop the eye before it reaches the objectionable sight. Situate the grass between what you don't want to see and the place from which it would most often be seen: the kitchen window, the patio, or the bay window.

Giant reed (*Arundo donax*)

In three years, a single clump of the giant reed will grow about five feet wide and twelve feet tall (in sun). Even though *Arundo* is not a dense grass, its striking presence will more than do the job of stopping the eye.

Ravenna grass (*Erianthus ravennae*)

Ravenna grass stays fairly low in clump, growing to only about four or five feet tall, but in early fall a well-established grass will shoot up as many as forty twelve-foot flower stalks.

Condensatus (*Miscanthus sinensis condensatus*)

Condensatus is another robust grass with early blooms that open pale gold and darken to a silken magenta color.

Silver Feather miscanthus (*Miscanthus sinensis* 'Silberfeder')

Feed it well and Silver Feather will quickly reach eight feet tall (in bloom) by about five feet wide. The spectacular "silver" plumes that appear in September are a beautiful bonus.

Clump bamboo (*Sinarundinaria nitida*)

Dainty and evergreen, with pale purple culms and bright green leaves, clump bamboo grows slowly to twenty feet tall and eight to ten feet in diameter. Hardy to $-20°F$, *Sinarundinaria nitida* is the hardiest of the non-running bamboos. Give it protection from strong winds and the afternoon sun. More difficult to find, another hardy clumping bamboo of handsome appearance is *Thamnocalamus spathaceus*.

For Low Hedges

Low hedges of ornamental grasses or combinations of grasses and perennials or grasses and evergreens may not screen out the world, but they do lend a comfortable sense of enclosure. They are particularly useful where an outdoor living area boasts a good view but suffers from too much openness. A low boundary of grasses and other plants raises the psychological comfort level within such an exposed place without obstructing the view.

Feather reed grass (*Calamagrostis acutiflora stricta*)

Feather reed grass comes up early, blooms early, and spends the rest of its days adorned with showy, very upright seeds. Mix it with mounding perennials or evergreens, mugo pine or junipers, for winter contrast when it's bright cream and gold.

Moor grass (*Molinia caerulea arundinacea* 'Windspiel')

Moor grass is wonderful rising out of blocks of perennials such as *Sedum* 'Autumn Joy' or low-growing goldenrods, to name only two of a hundred possibilities. The splendid, long, fine flower stalks are wonderful to watch as they bend and sway in constant motion. This is the plant to site next to a terrace, where it can be enjoyed from summer when the flower stalks first appear until it is too cold to sit outside.

Switch grass (*Panicum virgatum*)

Coddle switch grass a bit and it will grow dense and lustrous, sending up clouds of fine seeds in early fall. Use its lush density as a foil for angular perennials such as the white *Datura*, roses, or small trees.

Fountain grass (*Pennisetum alopecuroides*)

Fountain grass works well with just about any plant. Combined with tall, narrow evergreens such as the 'Skyrocket' junipers, or with showy shrubs such as *Fothergilla* or *Franklinia*, fountain grass creates a boundary planting that provides a sense of comfortable enclosure while remaining open to the view.

GRASSES FOR SPECIMENS AND CONTAINERS

Some ornamental grasses are dramatic, imposing, memorable. Placed sparingly in the garden like pieces of sculpture, these grasses work as extraordinary specimens. Unlike sculpture, however, an ornamental grass is never a set piece. It is dynamic, growing swiftly to voluminous proportions, changing color, and filling the garden with its sounds.

Any one of the big grasses can function as a specimen. Used alone, it breaks up an expanse of lawn or low-growing ground cover. Situated beside a path or driveway, it is a distinguishing accent. Upright in a field of annual or perennial flowers, it breaks up the horizontal plane with a dramatic vertical flourish.

Advantageous placement and companion plants that support rather than compete with a specimen grass enhance its impact in the garden. When adding accents, restraint is in order. Fewer specimens are definitely more effective than many. Less is more.

Size alone earns many grasses the role of specimen. But other qualities—intriguing architectural shapes, marvelous late season flowers, and unusual color—catapult lesser grasses into leading roles.

Large Specimen Grasses

Size, presence, and spectacular flowers endow these grasses with star quality.

Porcupine grass (*Miscanthus sinensis strictus*)

When size is combined with unusual color, a grass is destined for stardom. Such is the case with the most flamboyant of the miscanthus species, porcupine grass (*M. sinensis strictus*). A compact, upright, five-foot clump of yellow banded foliage, porcupine grass is similar in color to its near relative, zebra grass (*M. sinensis zebrinus*). Unlike zebra grass, which grows quickly and always seems to flop over its neighbors, porcupine grass is extremely upright and neat in appearance. It flares out a bit when it blooms in late fall. The characteristic yellow banding of both species is more pronounced in young specimens and grasses growing in full sun.

Ravenna grass *(Erianthus ravennae)*

Sometimes called northern pampas grass, Ravenna grass is nothing if not imposing—in bloom. Although the clump of Ravenna grass grows only about four to five feet high, its plumes, sent out in late summer, can reach fourteen feet. An established specimen of this dusty green grass sends up formidable flowers—forty or even fifty bushy blue-beige plumes.

Ravenna grass, with its somewhat irregular tousled foliage makes a good specimen in a naturalistic garden, where a less formal, less uniform grass works best. It has the reputation of disliking damp clay soils and, for this reason, one often sees it planted on slopes or mounds created specially for it. Mounds enhance its impact before bloom and afterward, when it dominates a garden vista.

Ravenna grass responds to good care with strong growth. Horticulturist and nurseryman Kurt Bluemel recommends two methods for curbing its growth if the gardener fears it may get out of hand: (1) Keep it "hungry" by not feeding it; (2) grow it in a sunken, bottomless five-gallon drum.

Giant reed *(Arundo donax)* and variegated giant reed *(Arundo donax variegata)*

Sheer size, a light glaucous blue-green color, and intriguing structure—bamboo-like segmented canes with broad, cleanly cut leaves—combine in the giant reed, an outstanding specimen grass. Because its leaves are spaced about nine inches apart, its effect is loose and open. Giant reed forms an interestingly shaped, irregular sculptural accent, rather than a dense mass. Give it lots of room and full sun, without which it tends to lean over its lower-growing neighbors. Canes grow to about twelve feet. Variegated *Arundo* is smaller, reaching only around eight or nine feet.

Giant miscanthus *(Miscanthus floridulus)*

More compact, upright, and dense than the giant reed and almost as tall as Ravenna grass, giant miscanthus grows to twelve feet and, where the climate is warm, blooms in October. Its broad, overlapping blades held on erect canes suggest a deep green waterfall. Giant miscanthus is bolder and less formal in habit than other miscanthus species and fits more easily into a naturalistic setting. Superb rising out of stones in a rock garden, it colors fleetingly apricot in fall before fading to a fine creamy winter color. By mid-

The giant reed (*Arundo donax*, at left) and feather reed grass (*Calamagrostis acutiflora stricta*, in seed) combine in the Japanese Garden at Brookside Gardens.

winter, the wind will have blown away most of the short leaves, but the canes remain for a strong vertical accent.

Condensatus *(Miscanthus sinensis condensatus)*

Full-figured condensatus grass, with its broad leaf blades, grows swiftly into a dense, stocky clump. Although it flares out in late summer, its foliage has more starch than other miscanthus species, so the clump develops into a broad but fairly erect fan shape. This broad and generous habit brings a sense of great mass and weight to a planting. Its powerful form counterbalances weighty and powerful garden elements like boulders or great expanses of stone.

Miscanthus condensatus blooms in August or early September, depending upon climate. When flowers first unfold, they are a pale, shimmering gold. Later they often take on a magenta cast.

Maiden grass *(Miscanthus sinensis* 'Gracillimus')

The name 'Gracillimus' says it all. Maiden grass is an elegant lady, the most graceful of all and, perhaps because of its extremely fine texture and even vase shape, it is also the most formal. Young specimens are especially regular. Their perfect vase shapes of finely striped blades seem to have been skillfully pruned to achieve such symmetry. In the slightest breeze, foliage stirs deep within the clump with the suppressed energy of a thoroughbred.

Because *Miscanthus sinensis* and its varieties and cultivars grow in a ring from the center outward, older specimens, lacking central support, may favor one side and lean toward it. To maintain a perfect and narrow vase shape, divide maiden grass when it becomes irregular, and expect a satisfactory new grass in the second year. For a specimen of lordly presence and impressive size, leave it alone for ten years or more and enjoy whatever eccentricities it exhibits.

Maiden grass blooms in October. Repeated frosts bleed out its green summer color, turning it to a bright, showy almond in winter.

Eulalia grass *(Miscanthus sinensis)*

Classic Eulalia grass falls midway between maiden grass and *Miscanthus sinensis condensatus* in size, shape, and texture. Its vase shape is a bit more robust than that of maiden grass, but more slender than the full-bodied condensatus. Broader leaf blades than those of maiden grass provide for distinct texture, making it a better choice for a naturalistic setting. Like maiden grass, its winter coloring alone would be reason enough to grow Eulalia grass. It blooms before maiden grass, fanning out when the magenta plumes appear.

Miscanthus sinensis 'Autumn Light'

There are many cultivars of *Miscanthus sinensis*, and many more will come to light as nurseries select for outstanding qualities. 'Autumn Light' is a good citizen. It gives gardeners great satisfaction because it doesn't do anything wrong. More compact and somewhat shorter than Eulalia grass, it doesn't need restraint, doesn't flop over (even in a heavy rain), blooms well, and is attractive in winter. Choose 'Autumn Light' as a specimen in a small dooryard or townhouse garden.

Small Specimen Grasses

The grasses listed below have star quality but manageable size. These specimen grasses won't overwhelm a small garden.

Spodiopogon sibiricus

Not a small grass, spodiopogon will grow five feet tall and four feet wide. Because of its rich, bamboo-like tropical texture and its ability to tolerate some shade, however, it is a good choice for a small, walled garden. It is complete unto itself by virtue of its attractive foliage, and the flowers that appear in late summer are a bonus. Plant spodiopogon in a bed of evergreen ground cover and cut back after frost when the leaves are shriveled and brown.

Molinia caerulea arundinacea 'Windspiel' and Molinia caerulea arundinacea 'Transparent'

All anyone needs to do to have kinetic sculpture in the garden is one 'Windspiel' plant and at least sixty-four square feet of yard—arranged eight feet square. The grass clump doesn't need much room, but the amazing flowers that appear at the ends of six- to seven-foot stems arching over the plant, bobbing and swaying in the air, do. This dancing grass contrasts a bushy clump of tousled ribbon-like foliage with long, elegant, hair-fine stems and flowers. In addition to plenty of room, 'Windspiel' needs a plain background—preferably dark, as with a row of evergreens—and no vertical competition for its flowers, which turn golden yellow in fall, if these are to be seen to best advantage. For those without a minimum of sixty-four square feet, there is the smaller cultivar 'Transparent.'

Quietly green all summer long, flame grass (*Miscanthus sinensis purpurascens*) sends up rose-colored flowers in the author's garden in August. The bed of threadleaf coreopsis, which blooms lemon yellow all summer, is a good companion for flame grass throughout the year.

At about the time that the dogwoods turn color, flame grass does likewise. It remains pumpkin-colored throughout the winter. The bed of coreopsis in which it is growing turns to a dark, smoky charcoal brown, contrasting with the grass all winter long.

Miscanthus sinensis 'Yaku Jima'

Growing only three to four feet tall, 'Yaku Jima' is a Japanese miniature form of Eulalia grass that is perfect for very small spaces. Foliage is dark green and upright and, although about the same size as that of Eulalia grass, looks somewhat more coarse because of the grass's small stature.

Flame grass (*Miscanthus sinensis purpurascens*)

Flame grass, a closet exhibitionist, exhibits three feet of medium green, erect foliage by mid-summer and no hint of its fiery fall personality. When pink fanlike flowers appear on eighteen-inch stems in late summer, anyone growing this grass can be well satisfied with its performance as a clean, attractive small grass with showy flowers, and that's that. And then, as the leaves and temperature fall, flame grass shows its true colors, turning a bright orangey red. After frost, the color fades just a bit but persists throughout the winter.

Foxtail grass (*Calamagrostis arundinacea brachytricha*)

Foxtail grass is grown for its enormously showy foxy inflorescences—two-foot-long, lavender-white fluffy flowers that appear in September and persist for two months transform this two-foot-high fan-shaped grass from innocuous nonentity into garden star. Once frost hits and the wind starts blowing, foxtail grass quickly loses its appeal and requires immediate cutting back. Nevertheless, foxtail grass provides a fall spectacle worth watching for.

Container Grasses

A pot of grasses does for patio or doorstep what a specimen does for the lawn or garden. It breaks monotony—softens an expanse of paving, adds a spot of interest, and presents an appealing focus. It also provides a good opportunity for us to try the untried. It's an easy and painless way to enter the world of grasses without turning a shovelful of soil.

Just about any grass can be grown in a container if its moisture needs are met, but some are especially promising. Fountain grass (*Pennisetum alopecuroides*), a plant for all places, not surprisingly looks great in a container. Other good container grasses include but are not restricted to those with unusual color or pendant habits.

Striped Eulalia grass (*Miscanthus sinensis variegatus*)

A riveting white-striped beauty grown in the ground or in a container, striped Eulalia grass is a bit smaller than the straight

Annual pennisetums, in this case *Pennisetum setaceum*, fill a clay pot in the Enid A. Haupt Garden of the Smithsonian Institution, on the north side of the National Museum of African Art.

species, reaching only about five feet tall. Leaf blades are longitudinally striped white and broad—very nearly the size of condensatus. Yet striped Eulalia appears altogether more delicate and less robust than either condensatus or Eulalia grass. Clean, green and white striped leaves arch into a graceful vase shape.

Annual fountain grass (*Pennisetum setaceum*)

Annual fountain grass is very similar and every bit as pretty as its perennial relative *P. alopecuroides,* and counts long-blooming, rose-tinted flowers among its charms. Arching leaf blades cascade over the edge of pots, adding a cool, graceful note to a terrace or doorway. Start this grass from seed and enjoy a long season of rosy bloom.

The annual pennisetum cultivar *P. setaceum* 'Atrosanguineum' has a more upright habit than *P. setaceum* and is a deep maroon-purple with wonderful seven-inch-long flowers. Other "red" pennisetums include 'Cupreum' and 'Rubrum.'

A potted garden of alternating fescues and ivy tops a wall in this Seattle garden. (Photo by Cynthia Woodyard)

Feathertop (*Pennisetum villosum*)

As easy to grow from seed as zinnias, *P. villosum* is striking in pots or plots. Chubby flowers are pure white and fluffy and borne on thirty-inch stems produced evenly throughout clumps of fine, pendant foliage.

Festuca species

The cool-season, gray-green fescues that are so splendid in bloom need a bit of tender, loving care afterwards. Especially in hot summer areas, move pots to a shady recuperation area, and snip off seed stalks when the fescue looks tired. By fall it will revive. Some people report great success after burning back dead foliage.

Switch grass (*Panicum virgatum*)

An easy-to-grow grass that isn't fussy about moisture, *Panicum virgatum* or one of its attractive and colorful cultivars makes an excellent and unexpected pot plant. The red forms, *P. virgatum* 'Rotstrahlbusch' or *P. virgatum* 'Haense Herms' are more compact

101

than ordinary switch grass, growing to only about three feet tall. In a spot where it receives at least four hours of sunshine each day, a young plant will stand erect and send up graceful sprays of delicate flowers in mid-summer: a potted prairie.

Japanese blood grass (*Imperata cylindrica* 'Red Baron')

Keep Japanese blood grass moist but well drained and, for best color, place the container where it will receive at least two to three hours of sunshine each day. Japanese blood grass glows red and grows to about eighteen inches tall. It will spread by slow rhizomes to fill a container.

GRASSES FOR THE PERENNIAL BORDER

Ornamental grasses are superb additions to a perennial border. They lengthen the border's season of show, adding volume and color before and after most perennial flowers bloom. Green grasses arbitrate between what might otherwise be strident colors, surrounding brightly colored flowering subjects with a soothing matrix of neutral green. Colored and variegated grasses enhance the effect of flowering plants. Throughout the year, they add a soft fullness that is especially effective around narrow, upright flowering subjects. In early spring, cool-season grasses peak and bloom before many perennials completely revive. Late in the season, when many perennials look tired, warm-season grasses are still fresh and green, and many have not yet begun to bloom. As winter approaches and other ornamentals wither to dried sticks, grasses retain volume and keep the garden from looking bare.

Cool-Season Grasses for the Perennial Border

These early-growing grasses flesh out the border in the early spring with much needed volume, providing companionship for the earliest flowers. Some to consider for early show are

☐ Bulbous oat grass (*Arrhenatherum elatius bulbosum variegatum*)
☐ Feather reed grass (*Calamagrostis acutiflora stricta*)
☐ Fescues (*Festuca* species)
☐ Blue hair grass (*Koeleria glauca*)
☐ Blue oat grass (*Helictotrichon sempervirens*)
☐ Velvet grass (*Holcus lanatus variegatus*)
☐ Mellic (*Melica ciliata*)
☐ Mellic (*Melica transylvanica*)
☐ Ribbon grass (*Phalaris arundinacea picta*)
☐ *Stipa gigantea*

Warm-Season Grasses for the Perennial Border

When perennial flowers pass their peak in late summer and fall, warm-season grasses keep the border looking fresh. Their fall blooms extend the flowering season and keep the border interesting long after most perennials have given up. The following grasses can be counted upon for a fresh and showy appearance in the late summer and fall garden:

☐ Sea oats (*Chasmanthium latifolium*)
☐ Foxtail grass (*Calamagrostis arundinacea brachytricha*)
☐ Lyme grass (*Elymus glaucus*)
☐ Ravenna grass (*Erianthus ravennae*)
☐ Japanese blood grass (*Imperata cylindrica* 'Red Baron')
☐ Giant miscanthus (*Miscanthus floridulus*)
☐ Flame grass (*Miscanthus purpurascens*)
☐ Eulalia grass (*Miscanthus sinensis*)
☐ Maiden grass (*Miscanthus sinensis* 'Gracillimus')
☐ Condensatus (*Miscanthus sinensis condensatus*)
☐ Fountain grass (*Pennisetum alopecuroides*)
☐ Annual pennisetum (*Pennisetum setaceum*)
☐ Feathertop (*Pennisetum villosum*)
☐ Indian grass (*Sorghastrum nutans*)
☐ Prairie cord grass (*Spartina pectinata aureo-marginata*)

Grasses for the Back of the Border

In a single season, large ornamental grasses do what it takes years for a hedge to do: They provide a flower border with between six and twelve feet of green background. When it is planted within the border, a large grass stops the eye—an especially useful feature where a change in color scheme occurs. When teamed with giant perennials like Joe Pye weed, *Boltonia*, Tartarian asters, or *Heracleum*, these giant grasses function within the border, adding one last, very tall layer.

Ravenna grass (*Erianthus ravennae*)

Ravenna grass grows into a large mound of cascading foliage. On a well-grown clump, fall flowers are numerous and spectacular, providing a grand finale to the border's progress. During the summer, Ravenna grass is wider than it is tall. In clump, it grows to about three and a half feet tall when established. For this reason, although its four- to five-foot width is space-consuming, it can occupy a place in the mid-border. By the time its twelve-foot flower stalks appear in fall, little else will offer distraction.

Giant miscanthus (*Miscanthus floridulus*)

Where there is no hedge or wall to back up a border, giant miscanthus, with its very upright habit and dark green foliage, is an excellent backdrop for tall flowers. White fanlike flowers of the giant miscanthus appear in fall.

Eulalia grass (*Miscanthus sinensis*)

Eulalia grass is a handsome subject for the back of the border all summer. Striking fall flowers are a bonus. Tall Tartarian asters, tall heleniums, and white *Boltonia* are proportionate companions to Eulalia and maiden grass.

Maiden grass (*Miscanthus sinensis* 'Gracillimus')

Like Eulalia grass, maiden grass provides a handsome green background for tall flowers at the back of the border. Its foliage is finer than that of Eulalia, and its flowers appear somewhat later. Within the border, it serves as a prominent but graceful accent.

Condensatus (*Miscanthus sinensis condensatus*)

Condensatus is a big grass for the back of the border whose flowers appear in very late summer before the other large grasses of the miscanthus tribe bloom.

Prairie cord grass (*Spartina pectinata aureo-marginata*)

Clean cascading foliage for the back of the border turns to bright yellow in fall.

Grasses for the Mid-Border

Grasses in the mid-border interact with flowering perennials. Their neutral green foliage acts both as a buffer between bright colors and a filler around angular flowering subjects. Plan for their winter colors as well as their summer appearance.

Feather reed grass (*Calamagrostis acutiflora stricta*)

Feather reed grass is one of the few early-blooming cool-season grasses that stay showy throughout the year—a very nearly permanent fixture in the border. By mid-spring, the foliage of feather reed grass is well developed. June-blooming flowers are delicate, open panicles, turning from white to beige-pink. These combine well with pink flowers. Lythrum is an outstanding companion. Upright, pale tan seeds form in July and are effective and attractive in winter until the grass is cut down in late winter or early spring.

Foxtail grass *(Calamagrostis arundinacea brachytricha)*

A neat, pincushion clump of summer foliage, useful for neutral separation of bright colors, gives no hint of foxtail grass's amazingly showy fall flowers. To augment the beauty of these ten-inch-long plumes, emerging in the palest shade of lavender and later turning to white and off-white, Edith Eddleman combines foxtail grass with pink *Lespedeza* and pink *Boltonia*.

Sea oats *(Chasmanthium latifolium)*

The handsome texture of its summer foliage is reason enough to grow this attractive, two-foot-tall bamboo-like plant. Wonderful fall seeds that dangle from delicate stems add to its charms.

Lyme grass *(Elymus glaucus)*

This gray-blue plant augments a blue color scheme and is a wonderful foil to creamy yellow and orange flowers like day lilies and butterfly weed. Lyme grass provides a long season of clean, drought-resistant, attractive blue foliage. John Greenlee combines lyme grass with agaves in beach plantings.

Blue oat grass *(Helictotrichon sempervirens)*

Larger than blue hair grass and most fescues, blue oat grass boasts blue foliage that is nearly evergreen and dramatic. *Helictotrichon*'s early blooms dance over the garden on long, arching stems. Blue oat grass is a good companion to lavender.

Mellic *(Melica transylvanica)*

This twenty-four-inch-tall, late spring-blooming plant provides a focus in the border just after the irises bloom. It holds onto its attractive white seed heads throughout the summer.

Flame grass *(Miscanthus sinensis purpurascens)*

Flame grass provides pleasant, bright green volume throughout the summer, when it produces silken fanlike flowers that turn from magenta to bright white. In fall, it turns color in concert with dogwoods. Its pale orange is striking behind *Sedum* 'Autumn Joy' and cream-colored chrysanthemums. As fall advances into winter, the grass turns a lovely autumn orange.

Splendid in the perennial border, grasses add tremendous volume, showy inflorescences, and subtle color. A spectacular *Stipa gigantea* dominates the left foreground in the border at the North Carolina State University Arboretum. Directly behind that is a variegated Eulalia grass *(Miscanthus sinensis variegatus)*. In the right foreground, blue lyme grass *(Elymus glaucus)* rises behind threadleaf coreopsis. The large grasses, starting at back row center, are zebra grass *(Miscanthus sinensis zebrinus)*, variegated arundo *(Arundo donax variegata)*, a Joe Pye weed, maiden grass *(Miscanthus sinensis* 'Gracillimus'). (Design: Edith Eddleman)

Switch grass *(Panicum virgatum)*

Use switch grass as a wonderful softener in the mid-border. Its seeds, produced in late summer, form beige-pink clouds around flowering plants. The color is wonderful with both orange and pink companions. The smaller growing cultivars 'Haense Herms,' 'Rotstrahlbusch,' and 'Rehbraun' add bright red fall color, while *P. virgatum* turns a lovely bright wheat color in winter.

Fountain grass *(Pennisetum alopecuroides)*

Fountain grass, useful in virtually every other garden situation, works splendidly in the border. Placement among other plants will hold the grass in a more erect position, but a position in the foreground allows stems and flowers to fall into the characteristic cascade. Its lovely cream-colored flowers, appearing in mid-summer, work well with the white form of the coneflower *(Echinacea purpurea)*. It also forms very long-lasting relationships with *Rudbeckia* 'Goldsturm,' *Sedum* 'Autumn Joy,' or P.G. hydrangeas. If *P. alopecuroides* is too large, try the smaller *P. alopecuroides* 'Hameln.'

A giant blue-green clump of Ravenna grass *(Erianthus ravennae)* and a bright green dog fennel break up the long border at the North Carolina State University Arboretum. (Design: Edith Eddleman)

Annual pennisetum *(Pennisetum setaceum)*

Annual pennisetum produces rose-colored flowers that are effective throughout the summer. Annual pennisetum is wonderful with pink forms of *Nicotiana*.

Feathertop *(Pennisetum villosum)*

Feathertop produces puffy cream-colored flowers all summer long. It is an excellent, bushy subject for an all-white border.

Indian grass *(Sorghastrum nutans)*

Copper-colored, silky flowers are borne above low clumps of foliage. Pair Indian grass with rust-colored chrysanthemums.

Stipa gigantea

Stipa's foliage revives early, but its spectacular summer flowers steal the show. Growing from a low, eighteen-inch clump, stipa's flowers are carried on five-foot stems. A cool-season grass, it may become dormant in late summer in hot summer climates. Choose late-blooming companions.

Grasses for the Front Border and for Edging

Small grasses for the front and edging of a border planting abound. Cool-season types frame the border and augment the show of bulbs. Evergreen grasses provide structure all year long.

Bulbous oat grass (*Arrhenatherum elatius bulbosum variegatum*)

Bulbous oat grass's clean, white-striped foliage is a fresh and attractive focus from early spring into summer. Summer flowers climax its show in the garden. Combine it with the deep green foliage and white flowers of candytuft in front of irises.

Fescues (*Festuca* species)

Many fescues begin to bloom in the lull between the last tulips and early perennials like Oriental poppies, with which they overlap. While a single flower is not showy enough to add to the bouquet, the effect of an entire plant covered with uniformly held flower stalks is that of a bouquet in the front of the border. Try fescues in combination with glaucous ground covers like creeping phlox, *Aurinia saxitalis*, *Cerastium*, or lamb's ears. They are excellent in a dry, sunny situation.

Japanese blood grass (*Imperata cylindrica* 'Red Baron')

Japanese blood grass is a good season-long source of bright red in the front of the border. It stays colorful through light frosts until hard frost turns it a brown-orange color. Bright red crocasmias, wine red cosmos, and chrysanthemums are superb companions to Japanese blood grass.

Blue hair grass (*Koeleria glauca*)

Like that of the fescues, blue hair grass's spring flower show adds early drama to the front of the border. Ice blue hedgehog-shaped plants are attractive sources of color, with or without flowers.

Velvet grass (*Holcus lanatus variegatus*)

Velvet grass, a perfect edging, is a low-growing, very dense, bright white and green striped cool-season grass. Try velvet grass with massed white tulips.

Mellic *(Melica ciliata)*

This small treasure provides a graceful cascade of early foliage and early summer flowers.

Ribbon grass *(Phalaris arundinacea picta)*

Ribbon grass provides color—variegated white and green foliage—virtually all season long. Ribbon grass is breathtaking with white or pastel astilbes.

GRASSES FOR SHADE

Most sedges and some grasses prefer shade. Other grasses grow best in full sun but tolerate considerable amounts of shade. Combining these shade-loving and shade-tolerant individuals yields enough material to stock a good-sized garden with variety and interest.

Bowles Golden grass (*Carex stricta* 'Bowles Golden') contrasts with *Agapanthus* in the Savill Garden in England. (Photo by Cynthia Woodyard)

The Sedges

The sedges, members of the genus *Carex*, provide abundant ground cover subjects. Virtually all will grow in light to full shade. There are small treasures—plants for small, bare, but closely observed spaces. The tiny six-inch-tall bird's foot sedge (*Carex ornithopoda variegeta*), the larger, eight-inch-tall *Carex conica marginata*, tousled green with a silvery stripe, and six-inch-tall blue-green black sedge (*Carex nigra*) are the sorts of plants that give a fine finish to the garden, adding rich texture with lush, handsome, but unobtrusive foliage.

Larger sedges like the Japanese silver sedge (*Carex morrowii variegata*) and one of its variegated forms, *C. morrowii aureo-variegata*, do well in light shade. Both grow a little over a foot tall, spreading at least as wide as they are tall. Both are semi-evergreen. Japanese silver sedge is predominantly dark green. Its name derives from fine white leaf margins along its arching foliage. *C. morrowii aureo-variegata* is predominantly creamy yellow. Leaves grow long and curl under, giving the plant a tousled tuffet-like appearance.

Growing twenty inches high, Bowles Golden grass (*C. stricta* 'Bowles Golden'), long a favorite in English gardens, serves as a great brightener in shade. (In the South, Bowles Golden grass can take more shade, in the North less.) The name is apt. It is a golden grass with just a hint of green. It looks like a spot of sunlight when grown along a shady path.

Two sedges that straddle the line between sun and shade are the palm sedge (*C. muskingumensis*) and the leatherleaf sedge (*C. buchananii*). The former looks good when planted in masses as a ground cover, growing to about eighteen inches tall. In that situation, it presents a delicate, feathery texture that is a wonderful contrast to stone paths and tree trunks. Leatherleaf sedge is unique in its cinnamon-brown-fading-to-drab-green color. Designer Edith Eddleman has combined it brilliantly with green and gold *Chrysogonum virginianum*, pale yellow crocuses, a pale cream form of *Kerria japonica*, and *Mahonia*.

Drooping sedge (*C. pendula*), striking in bloom, serves as a fine small, thirty-inch-tall specimen for a shady space. The long, arching, deep green, straplike leaves are semi-evergreen. Use drooping sedge as an accent over low ground cover.

Grasses for Half-Shade

In addition to the sedges, a number of grasses do best in shade and half-shade. Foremost among these are *Hakonechloa macra* and its variegated form *H. macra aureola*. Difficult to establish in hot summer areas, hakonechloa, a denizen of the mountains of Japan, rewards the persistent with a cascade of green or cream and green

At its best in a cool summer climate, variegated hakonechloa thrives in the Chatto Garden in England. (Photo by Cynthia Woodyard)

satiny foliage that is just as attractive after frost, when it has been turned to a golden wheat color.

Deschampsia caespitosa and its cultivars are better, more attractive plants for cool climates, where their unique flowers achieve their full potential. In hot summer areas, while flowers are a bit less showy, deschampsia does supply a virtually evergreen clump of deepest green.

Two fine subjects for half-shade are river oats (also called northern sea oats, *Chasmanthium latifolium*) and the variegated, green and white form of Eulalia grass (*Miscanthus sinensis variegatus*), which does well with morning sun. Attractive all by itself, river oats grows to three feet in clumps of graceful, bamboo-like foliage that are crowned in late summer with dangling, oatlike seeds. Attractive on the plant, the seeded stems are also used in bouquets.

Woodland and Cool-Climate Grasses

Place of origin is the best guide to placement of plants in the garden. Plants that hail from woodland situations, such as *Luzula pilosa, Luzula sylvatica,* and *Hystrix patula,* do well in shade. Likewise, plants native to very cool places do best in shade in warm climates. Among these are the tiny fescue *Festuca scoparia* 'Pic Carlit,' the spikey mellic M. *ciliata,* and golden grass (*Milium effusem aureum,* sometimes mistakenly called Bowles Golden grass), a wonderful bright yellow-green grass that luxuriates in the cool temperatures of early spring but browns out in hot, dry weather. The delicate clump bamboo *Sinarundinaria,* also called blue clump bamboo, and the large bamboo-like *Spodiopogon sibiricus* also belong in this category.

Sun-Loving but Shade-Tolerant Grasses

Other grasses prefer sun but tolerate shade by virtue of their truly strong constitutions. Switch grass (*Panicum virgatum*) and prairie cord grass (*Spartina pectinata aureo-marginata*) are two of these. Aggressive ribbon grass (*Phalaris arundinacea picta*) and sturdy giant miscanthus (M. *floridulus*), growing to eight feet, are vigorous sun-loving, but shade-tolerant subjects.

If in doubt, try out a grass in the shady spot in your garden. If, after a season, it does not thrive, move it until you find its optimum position. Sometimes you can minimize a sedge's or grass's need for shade by giving the plant increased moisture in a sunnier location. You can lighten shade that is too deep by trimming overhead trees. Because there are so many variables, it is impossible to lay down hard and fast rules about sun and shade. Morning sun is cooler than afternoon sun. Plants, in general, tolerate more shade in the South than in the North. The best way to find out for certain how much shade (or sun) a grass needs in your garden is to try it.

GRASSES FOR BOUQUETS AND ARRANGEMENTS

If for no other reason, grow grasses to provide material for summer and fall bouquets.

Perennials

Two or three culms of the graceful maiden grass mixed with a bouquet of summer flowers are wonderously dramatic accents. After a year or two in the garden, most grasses are so thick and full that they provide a ready and generous source of filler and accent material for summer bouquets. Grasses with broad blades like *Arundo* and *Miscanthus sinensis condensatus* are good in dried flower bouquets. *Arundo* flowers are magnificent—almost a foot long and exotic-looking.

The flowers of fountain grasses are generously produced and work well in fresh and dried arrangements. To keep the pennisetum flowers from shattering, spray with the cheapest hairspray available

Ornamental grasses are a reliable source of interesting material for bouquets and flower arrangements. Here the fine seed heads of switch grass *(Panicum virgatum)* are a delicate balance to yellow flowers. (Design: Allie Uyehara)

Fresh flowers combine in Ikebana with the inflorescences of condensatus *(Miscanthus sinensis condensatus)* and fountain grass *(Pennisetum alopecuroides)*. (Design: Sheila Advani)

(the cheaper the spray, the greater the lacquer content). The silken fans of miscanthus varieties change quickly inside. To retard and somewhat restrain their curling and opening to off-white, use hairspray liberally.

Other outstanding grasses for bouquet-making include foxtail grass (*Calamagrostis arundinacea brachytricha*), whose foxtail-shaped flowers open to the palest shade of lavender; the late summer flowers of *Spodiopogon sibiricus*; the bottle brush summer seed heads of bottle brush grass (*Hystrix patula*); the early summer flowers of feather reed grass (*Calamagrostis acutiflora stricta*); and the light

Hare's tail grass (*Lagarus ovatus*) provides material for dried winter bouquets. (Original drawing reprinted from *Growing and Decorating with Grasses* with the kind permission of Peter Loewer.)

green bamboo-like leaves and interesting fall seed heads of sea oats *Chasmanthium latifolium).*

Annuals

"Annual grasses," states Peter Loewer, "do well anywhere." A much-published author, illustrator, and gardener who has written about ornamental grasses since 1976, when his book *Growing and Decorating with Grasses* appeared, Mr. Loewer grows many annual grasses in his garden in Cochecton Center, New York. He says that

Little quaking grass *(Briza minor)* and the larger quaking grass *(Briza maxima)* are two of Peter Loewer's favorites for summer bouquets. (Original drawing reprinted from *Growing and Decorating with Grasses* with the kind permission of Peter Loewer.)

Quaking Grass
Briza maxima

Little Quaking Grass
Briza minor

"many take the heat of an American summer with ease. The only problem I've ever had is with grasshoppers eating the foliage; they leave ragged tears in the leaves."

Mr. Loewer likes "a mix of annual grasses in a cutting garden to be used for fresh and winter bouquets." He finds that the best source for annual grass seeds "are English seed companies and various rock garden societies" that hold seed exchanges for their members.

His favorite annual grasses are: "Cloud grass (*Agrostis nebulosa*), an annual that I use around the garden and often in fresh flower arrangements. Quaking grass, both *Briza maxima* and *B. minor*, two annuals that I use throughout the perennial beds. Hare's-tail (*Lagarus ovatus*) is used in masses as a garden accent, then collected for winter bouquets. Goldentop (*Larmarkia aurea*) is used as an edging in the border. (I alternate it with Alpine strawberries.) Feather top (*Pennisetum villosum*) is spectacular, but the plants must often be tied up, as the blossoms are heavy."

Peter Loewer harvests some of his grasses for dried flower bouquets. He explains his method:

"To properly gather the blossoms, pick the stems on a dry and sunny day after the dews of morning have evaporated. Try to find flowers that have not completely opened and cut the stems as long as you can—they can always be trimmed later. To dry the grasses, strip off any excess leaves and tie small bunches of stems tightly together and hang them upside down on wire coat hangers, leaving plenty of space between for air circulation."

7. MEADOWS, PRAIRIES, AND NATIVE GRASSES

A NATURALLY OCCURRING meadow or prairie—or one that has been restored—is a complex mixture of forbs and grasses, a climax community in which a succession of different native plants bloom in waves. Even when a meadow has been carefully started and maintained by the hand of man, the end result is the arrival at a state as close to nature as possible, in which human intervention becomes less frequent. Once established, such a meadow looks natural. Plants grow in random patterns, and their individual effects are subservient to the effect of the whole.

A stylized meadow is different. Called "meadow" because it is composed of herbaceous plants that are roughly the same height, it looks neater and more formal than a natural meadow. Clearly designed and clearly man-made, it is also more suitable for small yards, neighborhood situations where weed ordinances preclude natural meadows, or places where a flowing meadow-like ground cover of herbaceous plants fits into the setting.

The climax growth of many different groups of plants that characterizes a real meadow or prairie is carefully orchestrated in a stylized one. Instead of native plants, however, the mock meadow employs the same kind of ornamental bulbs and plants that grow in the garden border. Having been bred for ornamental qualities such

ABOVE: Wild grasses and red poppies in a field in France. (Photo: Cynthia Woodyard)

as bushy habit or heavy bloom, ornamental plants tend to be larger and showier than many natives. When we use them in a mock meadow to create successive bursts of bloom, these plants remain individually prominent.

CHOOSING PLANTS FOR THE STYLIZED MEADOW

In a stylized meadow, group ornamentals of one kind together—with the exception of bulbs—rather than intersperse them in the random patterns found in nature. Both because they are showy ornamentals and because their effect is magnified by massing, when a particular group comes into bloom it has great impact. A large number of one kind of plant blooming is a grand spectacle, carefully planned into the meadow. Unlike the gentle, subtle color variations of a natural meadow, bloom is distinct, prominent, and showy in the stylized one.

In addition to the uniform splash of many plants of the same kind blooming at once, there are subtle side effects. Great numbers of one kind of plant before and after bloom provide great blocks of texture for interest and a uniform, finished look to the planting.

The height of plants to be included is an important consideration. Although heights can increase as the growing season proceeds, they should be roughly (though not exactly) the same at any one time for an overall meadow-like appearance. In places with an obvious center or back, like a planted island or driveway turnaround, position taller plants in the center. If the mock meadow is located at the edge of a property—for example, the back third of a rectangular backyard—place taller plants in back.

For good development, space plants at correct intervals. Very close spacing tends to force plants to grow or stand taller. Floppy plants in big blocks will hold each other up.

Nothing sets off any meadow better than evergreens. The ideal situation is an evergreen screen on the edge of the meadow, but an isolated pine in the background or evergreens growing here and there within the meadow are wonderful foils to masses of herbaceous plants. In winter, the contrast between herbaceous plants—particularly grasses—and evergreens is striking.

If there is no existing boundary between meadow and other planted areas (for example, a walk or a driveway), it's a good idea to add one to define the edges clearly. Adding a walk, edging, transition plants, or a border of shrubs—including evergreen shrubs—will frame the meadow.

Accent plants add height or a splash of color to break up the monotony dramatically. But not all grasses work. *Arundo* and *Miscanthus floridulus* are probably too tall. They would look out of proportion in a stylized meadow of plants two to three feet tall. Those with shorter clumps but very long flower stalks, such as *Erianthus* and *Molinia*, perform beautifully.

A field of fountain grasses (*Pennisetum alopecuroides*) at Richard Simon's Bluemount Nurseries in Monkton, Maryland, remains showy throughout the winter. Fountain grass is an excellent choice for a stylized meadow.

Map out your meadow by season. Many early-blooming bulbs and plants disappear by mid-summer. Choose plants for interest in all four seasons.

Late Winter to Early Spring

The earliest bulbs—winter aconites, snowdrops, *Crocus tomasinianus* (spreads rapidly), *Chionodoxa* (spreads rapidly), giant crocus—are wonderfully welcome harbingers of spring. Their small bulbs require relatively shallow planting and fit easily in the spaces between other bulbs and perennials. Cut down winter grasses early enough to enjoy these bulbs.

Spring

Daffodils and early-blooming species of tulips announce that spring is official. Position their bulbs between perennials or plant

119

summer-blooming annual grasses and flowers after they have bloomed.

Mid- to Late Spring

Large bulbs like Darwin tulips and Persian alliums and perennials like Oriental poppies (plants disappear in summer), Shasta daisies, and early-blooming grasses mark the transition from spring to summer. *Melica ciliata* and *Melica transylvanica*, *Festuca*, *Helictotrichon*, and *Calamagrostis arundinacea stricta* are grasses that provide early show in a stylized meadow.

Early to Mid-Summer

Giant alliums, day lilies, lilies, threadleaf coreopsis, purple and white coneflowers, yarrow, and *Rudbeckia fulgida* 'Goldsturm' are colorful subjects for a stylized meadow in early summer. Combine them with grasses like *Calamagrostis arundinacea stricta*, *Pennisetum alopecuroides*, *Pennisetum caudatum*, *Panicum*, *Sesleria*, and *Helictotrichon*. Interplant these grasses with Turk's cap lilies.

Tawny in October, *Molinia caerulea arundinacea* 'Windspiel' (at left) and a blooming miscanthus rise above a field of lavender in the Rosenberg garden on Long Island. (Design: Oehme, van Sweden & Associates, Inc.)

Late Summer to Fall

As the growing season progresses, plan for late summer interest. Plant long-blooming purple and white coneflowers, *Sedum* 'Autumn Joy,' chrysanthemums, and fall-blooming asters. *Miscanthus sinensis purpurascens* and *Panicum virgatum* 'Rotstrahlbusch' and the large accent grasses (*Miscanthus* species) are late bloomers.

Winter

Select grasses with good winter color for winter show. Plant almond-colored *Pennisetum* and *Sporobolus*, wheat-colored *Panicum* and *Sorghastrum*, almond *Miscanthus sinensis*, and soft orange *Miscanthus sinensis purpurascens*. Although grasses are the mainstay of a stylized meadow in winter, a few perennials have winter presence. The smoky gray foliage of the threadleaf coreopsis retains volume, and the copper-colored seed heads of *Sedum* 'Autumn Joy' remain prominent. *Rudbeckia fulgida* 'Goldsturm' bears very deep charcoal-brown seed heads.

Late Winter/Very Early Spring

Cut back grasses and perennials in preparation for the earliest bulbs.

A Blue-Gray Meadow

A very low meadow in misty shades of blue and gray is another delightful possibility in a sun-baked, well-drained spot. Blue-gray grasses like the fescues, *Koeleria*, *Helictotrichon*, and *Elymus* form the matrix of the meadow while taller variegated *Miscanthus* 'Morning Light' provides a subtle accent. Augment the blue theme with blue to mauve flowering perennials like catmint, *Perovskia*, and lamb's ears. Use evergreen lavender and santolina for form in winter. Designer Benedikt Wasmuth adds splashes of color to glaucous plants with low-growing *Sedum* 'Ruby Glow.'

NATIVE GRASSES IN NATURAL MEADOWS AND PRAIRIES

The 1987 catalog from Plants of the Southwest says it best: "See and grow your native grasses. They will bring you closer to the world around you. And ease of care for your land can only come with the re-establishment of what grows there naturally."

Many native grasses are used as ornamentals in traditional garden applications—as flower borders, ground covers, or specimens. But the reverse is not true. Exotic ornamental grasses cannot serve in the same way as indigenous plants in restoring native landscapes, because they come from other continents, other countries, other states, and other climates. They can never reconstitute the native landscape except in their own place of origin.

When indigenous grasses are used to recreate a native landscape—for example, a prairie—the emphasis shifts from the grass as a purely ornamental entity to the grass as a part of a larger scheme. "Prairie," the French word for meadowland, has come to mean a stretch of native grassland—once the predominant vegetation of vast stretches of the Mississippi basin. "Meadow" commonly refers to a field of wildflowers and grasses, often a clearing that is cut for hay. Meadows and prairies are complex communities of grasses and forbs in which a single grass is only a minute part of that community. It is the appearance of the whole community working together and how well it fits into its surroundings that we find beautiful and desirable, not the individual grass.

The goal of a prairie/meadow restoration is to mix together native plants—grasses and forbs—in such a way that, once established, it will continue on its own with only minimal human intervention. It is an attempt to recreate nature the way it used to be. In the United States, the coming of Europeans, large-scale agriculture, and urban development disrupted a landscape that "only 150 years ago . . . stretched as far as the eye could see in many parts of America's heartland," states ecologist Neil Diboll in "Prairie Plants and Their Use in the Landscape," adding, "Today, it is considered to be one of the rarest plant associations on the continent." A myriad of exotic species, extensive development, and changes in the water table contributed to the decline of native grasslands.

What is the point of recreating prairies—of going back in time environmentally? "Originally," says Diboll," prairie plantings were installed by ecologists whose primary interest was to preserve these plants from impending extirpation." Once people saw the first prairie restorations, however, they found other reasons to restore native vegetation.

"There is a hunger for something besides these predictable, nearly unchanging landscapes," states Dr. Darrel Morrison, of the University of Georgia's School of Environmental Design, who is noted for his prairie restorations. He notes "growing interest on many people's part to break with tradition." Instead of the customary year-round green-lawn-and-green-shrubs approach to landscaping, native landscaping offers something different and more dynamic. Morrison adds, there is a "fit into the surrounding natural landscape" and "seasonal diversity with rich variety of colors, textures, movement."

For eyes accustomed to the distinct lines, static greens, and brilliant flower colors of a more formal traditional approach, land-

Once established, prairie grasses withstand extremes of heat and cold, retain volume in winter, and serve as the matrix for the fleeting show of prairie forbs. Here, cord grass (*Spartina*) turns bright yellow in early fall at the St. Louis Botanic Garden's prairie restoration.

A view of the North American high prairie, with the Rocky Mountains looming in the distance.

scaping with natives presents a quiet kind of beauty. The source of this beauty is based on appropriateness to site and climate. Understated, appropriate, spontaneous, harmonious, some reflection and rethinking of notions of beauty may be required to appreciate its fine distinctions. Designing with native plants requires greater sensitivity and an acceptance of the subtlety of the native palette.

California native plant enthusiast Judith Lowry, of Larner Seeds, wrote of a mind-expanding experience after a stiff climb up to a mountain meadow. "We were initially disappointed to discover that only two flower species were in bloom at that time. It took a while for us to realize the richness of possibility that was offered here. A pool of rich blue lupines with a few scarlet paintbrushes in the middle was delightful in a different way from a random scattering of lupines and paintbrushes, a fairly even mixture of red and blue."

The riot of color we have come to expect in a flower border is not a natural phenomenon, as Ms. Lowry points out in "Notes on Natural Design." "Fifteen different species all blooming at once rarely occurs in nature, and as we became more discerning, we began to relish more subtle combinations involving limited numbers of species."

A mountain meadow may not have as many plants blooming at one time as a garden border, but any meadow has other delightful compensations. Beginning in spring, whole colonies of flowers bloom in successive counterpoint to the great encompassing green of the grasses. As spring-flowering plants complete their life cycle, they may go dormant, but they are swiftly eclipsed by later summer- and, finally, fall-blooming plants. As the season progresses, the forbs grow taller to compete for space and light.

In late fall, when perennial plants wither and become unsightly in a garden border, the forbs within a prairie or meadow community wither as well. But their browns, golds, coppers, and rusts are repeated in pleasing fall-colored patterns throughout the meadow, and they are supported by a matrix of grasses that do not lose their volume after frost. Instead of being diminished by the passing of the growing season, the meadow enters into another season of show.

In winter, fall colors fade to browns and shades of winter white, and the meadow embarks on yet another beautiful and seasonally appropriate phase. Using grasses in a meadow or prairie planting extends the landscape's period of interest far beyond just the flowering season. In summer, grasses are cool green filler for the color of the forbs. In fall and winter, as the forbs wither into earth-toned patterns, grasses retain their volume and turn pleasing and seasonally fitting colors.

Another reason to use grasses in a meadow or prairie setting is what Dr. Darrel Morrison calls "the ecological/resource conservation reason." He states, "Natives are suited to the region, and, if planted in the right micro-environment, require minimal support." Plants native to a particular area have had millennia in which to adapt to that climate and all that it offers in terms of insects, rainfall, sun, temperature, and winds. To survive in their native place they don't require pesticides, fungicides, and supplemental water, and that makes them ecologically sound choices.

Joyce Powers, of CRM Ecosystems, Inc., a company that specializes in restoring or reconstructing native ecosystems—particularly prairies and wetlands—believes that when properly selected and established, "native grasses do not require fertilizer or water and they provide habitat for wildlife." She adds that they will "grow in full sun and poor soils, restore worn out farm land, and [are] low-maintenance once established."

Low maintenance requirements are another very good reason for choosing a prairie or meadow planting, particularly in a rural or semi-rural setting. But the low-maintenance part comes in only after the meadow or prairie is established. And establishing this type of plant community is as much a matter of planning, work, soil preparation, and nurturing as establishing a lawn or a perennial border.

There is the mistaken idea—perhaps it is wishful thinking—that because this is a "wild" planting, one has only to scatter the seeds from a canned meadow mix wherever a meadow is desired and then

This meadow on Long Island was recently seeded to produce a show of wildflowers. Yearly mowing to remove small trees, brambles, and vines is necessary upkeep in a meadow planting.

sit back and wait for nature to take over. If this were true, then all of America's roadsides and fields would be covered with meadows of native plants. In fact, the aggressive exotic species, small trees, and brambles that we see growing in these untended areas are the same plants that we have to contend with when we plant a prairie or meadow.

A Meadow from Seed

In some parts of the country, the most economical way to start a meadow in a large area is first to eliminate existing vegetation completely and then to sow seeds. Neil Diboll and Brian Bader, of Prairie Nursery in Westfield, Wisconsin, which not only sells native American prairie wildflowers and grasses but offers landscape consultation, vary their approach for removing existing vegetation to suit the situation. Because a meadow is a perennial crop, Mr. Bader says, "the real effort goes into soil preparation. The reason for a heavy emphasis on soil preparation and the destruction of weeds is that newly sown native perennials will spend their first year developing root growth, while their above-ground growth is slight and would be swiftly overtaken by existing weeds."

"Every situation is specific," states Mr. Diboll. He adds, "If the site of a future prairie was previously in lawn, it is given a single treatment with a herbicide. If it was under agricultural cultivation in the previous year and shows no evidence of perennial weeds, it is simply seeded, following control of annual weeds just prior to planting." But if the area was an old field with a good crop of perennial weeds, they recommend three treatments with herbicide over the course of a year: one in early summer, one in mid- to late summer, and one in fall to destroy early, mid-season, and late-season weeds. In some instances, a third treatment may not be necessary. The following spring, however, they recommend "controlling newly germinated weed seeds with a further application of herbicide or by light cultivation before the weeds get big. Then the site is seeded."

Neil Diboll emphasizes, however, that "there is no cut and dried cookbook for this." There are three main variables: "soil type, existing perennial weeds," and "past land use—what is in the weed seed bank?" Mr. Diboll thinks that in the long run it is easier "to put the work behind you" by proper site preparation. He says, "It is time-consuming at the outset, but it puts the landscaper in control of the planting's composition and development. A specific association of plants in specific spots can be created in this way."

Seeding a meadow or prairie has to take place at the right time for both the plants involved and in terms of climate. Cool- and warm-season grasses germinate under different soil temperatures.

Warm-season grasses need warm soil to germinate. Mr. Diboll recommends late spring to early summer planting for them (between May 1 and July 1 in southern Wisconsin). On the other hand, cool-season grasses like the beautiful prairie dropseed (*Sporobolus heterolepis*) require cool soils and spring planting.

"Prairie forbs," says Mr. Diboll, "are highly variable in their germination patterns." Each needs a special set of conditions in order to sprout and grow. "Many," he adds, "require 'moist stratification' [a period of moist chilling] or overwintering in the soil to break seed dormancy. Others must be scarified [the seed's outer surface must be scratched or chipped] or treated with heat. Others germinate reliably with no special treatment. Most require warm weather, but some will only germinate during cool weather. Some germinate only in spring, others in spring or fall." He adds, "Many prairie seeds will remain viable in the soil for years, and will germinate on their own schedule when conditions are correct."

Once the future prairie has been seeded, Mr. Diboll says he seldom irrigates—even if the soil is as dry as powder. He waits for rain. "Don't worry about these plants," he says. "When it rains, they'll come up." In a normal year, Diboll can count on about thirty inches of rain in his area.

In other parts of the country, rain is seasonal and not nearly as profuse. In California and other parts of the Southwest, "we may get our last rain in April or May and it may be September before it rains again. There can be five months with no rain," says Judith Lowry, of Larner Seeds in Bolinas, California. She adds, "In a lot of ways, it's a dormant season and *some* natives will die if they're watered at this time." Heat and humidity foster the growth of a fungus that is lethal for some native plants.

Where rain is seasonal, seeds should be sown in fall. Ms. Lowry recommends that "the water-conscious gardener can take advantage of seeds' natural cycle, planting when the winter rains have begun. The seeds will germinate and make good growth during the rainy winter and explode into bloom when the sun comes out in the spring."

A Meadow by Letting the Grass Grow

In many parts of the East, water is plentiful. Summers can be hot and humid, fostering rapid, rampant growth. The problem for those wishing to grow a meadow is that the earth remembers its long history as a deciduous forest and more willingly supports that kind of plant community. If a meadow is left uncut for more than a year or two, trees come up swiftly. In five years an uncut meadow will become a forest.

"Everything wants to go back to deciduous forest," says Joanna

Reed, of Longview Farm in Malvern, Pennsylvania, who has maintained a meadow for fifteen years. She began, not by plowing and seeding the bare ground, but by managing what was there as a meadow and by augmenting it. In other words, she let the grass grow and cut out unwanted plants as they appeared. She also seeded in desirable ones. Augmenting, she says, can also be done by plugging in additional plants.

She remembers having to remove young hawthornes by hand in the early years. Now the most frequently found weed trees are "sassafrass and oaks along the edge."

"I wouldn't dare not to mow it," she says. She mows her meadow twice each year, once in the middle of summer and again in fall or late winter. "I find that by mowing late in July, the early things will have gone to seed." She has also discovered that this early mowing doesn't seem to bother late-blooming forbs like asters that bloom on shorter stems. In some ways, she thinks the lower meadow is more attractive because it is easier to see. The later mowing is done in time to enjoy the appearance of early low-growing violets and wild strawberries in the spring.

"It doesn't have the impact of a seeded meadow," says Ms. Reed. Nevertheless, over the years she has had good success with a number of showy wildflowers. Her best success was with *Penstemon,* which "found its own way" and blooms showily each year. "*Geranium maculatum* just came" and produces great splashes of pink each year. "Goldenrod was at the lower end [of the meadow] and it has moved up and may choke things out.

"Asters and white yarrow and daisies all hold their own," she says. "*Asclepias* (butterfly weed) is coming back, but I wouldn't say fast. It has gone from two plants to twenty." She has started butterfly weed from seed in flats "to try to get a few colonies going."

Over the fifteen years Ms. Reed has maintained her meadow she has observed that it is not a static entity. For example, she thinks that the percentage of grasses has gradually diminished. Poverty grass, a denizen of poor soils, has vanished as organic material from the mown meadow has enriched the soil. In addition, she has observed that once a plant finds its ideal growing conditions, it takes off. She planted *Penstemon digitalis* in two areas where it has continued to come up, but has noticed that it came on its own in a third area, where the patch is four times the size of either of the first two.

"I am always trying to find the place the plant likes—its ideal location." To provide greater variety in the available locations, she has cut paths through the meadow in hopes of encouraging plants that like a more open situation to grow along the verges.

The appropriateness of her method for the East has been borne out in a meadow at the National Arboretum in Washington, D.C.,

Started by "just letting the grass grow," this meadow with blooming swamp milkweed at the National Arboretum in Washington, D.C., is maintained by annual mowing and selectively removing unwanted vegetation.

Moisture-loving forbs and cattails thrive in a low spot at the National Arboretum's meadow.

where, again, a field was simply allowed to grow. Unwanted weeds, seedling trees, and vines were selectively removed. After several years, plants like ragweed, which need bare soil to germinate, were being shaded out and desirable species—daisies, black-eyed Susan, swamp milkweed, and asters—were providing showy blooms over a long season.

A Meadow from Transplants

It is also possible to establish a meadow or prairie by destroying existing vegetation and setting out plants. This method is faster but more expensive. Bader and Diboll recommend a 50:50 ratio of grasses and forbs placed at one to a square foot for good flower color. Flowering forbs give color to the planting, but it is the grasses that give it cohesiveness, serving as a textural matrix. Diboll sees the grasses as "the fabric of the meadow that holds things together and serves as a counterpoint to the brighter, showier flowers."

In choosing plants, Diboll observes that "regionality is extremely important. What works in the Northeast or Midwest doesn't necessarily work in the West or Southwest. Plant material should be selected according to its adaptability to region.

"The source of both plants and seeds," he adds, "is important because there is tremendous variety—regional variation—within a species." While both latitude and longitude are factors in regional variation, Diboll thinks the effect of latitude is far more dramatic. "It has," he says, "something to do with how a plant paces its season, which is based on day length. For this reason, material should come from as close by as possible—especially in terms of latitude."

Caring for a Meadow

Even when the plants are chosen for a specific region, they may need special care until they are established. Judith Lowry offers this advice for setting out California natives in California: "All native plants, no matter how drought tolerant, will require irrigation of one inch per week during the first dry season after they are planted out."

Once the meadow is established, Brian Bader says, "it's a low-maintenance planting. All you have to do is mow it and rake it in the spring, fertilize maybe, and water if it's convenient to increase the production of blooms."

"Established" means that seeds have sprouted, plants are well past the critical seedling stage, and a plant has developed a root system in place. It is then that the virtues of drought-resistant California natives or prairie plants like big bluestem (*Andropogon gerardi)* or switch grass *(Panicum virgatum),* whose roots go down twelve feet or more into the earth, become evident. No matter what the climate has to offer, these plants continue to grow and thrive. "This is what native planting is all about," says Neil Diboll. Native grasses possess a beauty perfectly fitted into their environment. They are environmentally sound and require low maintenance.

Darrel Morrison sees a natural progression to the appreciation of native meadows and prairies. "The use of ornamental grasses by some talented designers has opened a lot of people's eyes to the esthetic value of them," he remarks. "The next step is to select and use native grasses that are perhaps a bit more subtle; then the next step is to use them in natural community-like groupings."

GROWERS' FAVORITE NATIVE GRASSES

The growers of native grasses enthusiastically support their plants. Some growers feel that these native grasses belong in garden situations as well as in meadows. Meredith Clebsch, of Native Gardens in Greenback, Tennessee, says that although she prefers "natural landscapes and gardens that blend with nature, in a more formal garden, I think [grasses] give a much needed texture that in most cases is very easy to care for." An added dividend to grasses in the garden, she says, is that they attract "birds and other wildlife. When [grasses are] left uncut, the birds find cover and, of course, seed." She adds, "Look around. Grasses and flowers are always together!"

Ms. Clebsch recommends the following native grasses for gardens:

River oats, or sea oats *(Chasmanthium latifolium)*

"River oats are tolerant of dry soil and some shade. Some gardeners report river oats to be aggressive in rich soils, though we have not had such a problem. It is especially attractive on slopes in the fall where the seed heads can easily be seen. They make useful additions to dried arrangements."

Woolly broomsedge *(Andropogon glomeratus)*

"Woolly broomsedge needs a moist site—even slightly wet will do. Imagine the golden brown tones of common broomsedge in the fall, then multiply the fluffy seedhead by about four times and you have woolly broomsedge. Even after the seeds have flown, the remaining heads are very interesting left in the yard or brought into the house."

Indian grass (*Sorghastrum nutans*)

"Indian grass is a tall, slender clump with stems reaching about six feet. It does well in poor soils—cut banks are a common habitat—and will also tolerate open shade. Best used in groups, individual plants do not take up much space, two to three feet usually, and so may be used in most gardens."

California Native Grasses

"The native California bunchgrasses are valuable for erosion control, mass plantings on banks, as an important component of the wildflower meadow, perennial cover for vineyards and orchards, and last but certainly not least, to restore the beautiful and complex grasslands of California," says Judith Lowry. Her favorite California native is California fescue, described in her words below.

Cathy Johnson, of the Johnson Seed Company in Woodacre, California, is also partial to the native grasses of the area. She thinks that "people should know [that native grasses] have a wide range of uses: as animal forage, rangeland, as ornamentals, and for soil erosion control. [They] need little water and are perennials that can live for as long as one hundred years." One of her favorite California natives is purple needlegrass.

California fescue (*Festuca Californica*)

"California fescue is a lovely blue-green bunchgrass with blades to two feet and graceful flower stalks to five feet high. It is easy to grow and ornamental. Drought tolerant, it is one of the bunchgrasses that will grow in sun or shade. Its fountainlike clumps make a stunning design statement on a bank or in a clearing in the trees."

Purple needlegrass (*Stipa pulchra*)

Purple needlegrass is a perennial bunchgrass of slopes and open ground, with long and narrow blades, growing two to three and a half feet tall in sun. Cathy Johnson considers *Stipa pulchra* to be "one of the major species of the California grasslands."

OPPOSITE: Golden grass (*Milium effusum aureum*) blooming in Cynthia Woodyard's Portland, Oregon, garden. (Photo: Cynthia Woodyard)

A CLOSE-UP
OF GRASSES

8. PERENNIAL GRASSES, SEDGES, HEDGES, AND REEDS

T HE SELECT GROUP of perennial grasses, sedges, and reeds in this chapter have been chosen for outstanding ornamental qualities and overall garden worthiness. Each listing briefly describes the grass, notes whether it grows during warm or cool seasons, and rates its hardiness, expressing this information as a zone, as in "hardy in Zone 5." This means that the grass will survive the winter cold in zones 5, 6, 7, and 8, but may not do so in Zone 4. (To locate your garden's zone, see the United States Department of Agriculture's map in Appendix C. For quick reference, information on size, season of growth, hardiness, flowering time, and other characteristics has been compressed into a chart, located in Appendix D.)

In this close-up of perennial grasses, sedges, and reeds, plants are listed alphabetically by botanical name. In most cases, common names are also mentioned.

Yellow foxtail grass (*Alopecurus pratensis aureus*)

Yellow foxtail grass is a softly striped, yellow-green cool-season grass, hardy to Zone 6, that is at its best in cool weather. Native to Europe and Asia, it grows to about a foot in height and blooms in spring. Yellow foxtail grass likes a rich, moist soil, where it will

ABOVE: **The variegated form of** *Arundo donax*

135

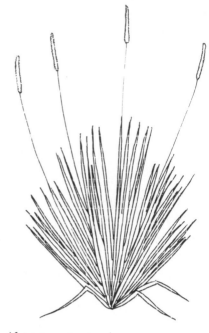

Alopecurus pratensis aureus

form an attractive clump in two to three years. It is especially attractive used in groups as a colorful ground cover.

Little bluestem (*Andropogon scoparius*, syn. *Schizachrium scoparium*)

Andropogon scoparius is a native American prairie grass with good drought and cold tolerance. A warm-season grass, it is hardy in Zone 4—and probably hardy in Zone 3. Its common name derives from the blue color present at the base of the clump. Upright foliage reaches about thirty inches and can be touched red. After frost, little bluestem turns a rich orangey wheat color. There are a number of other native bluestem grasses that are not on the market as ornamentals yet. These will become more desirable as native plant gardeners and those interested in low-water-use landscaping begin to use grasses. Among these are big bluestem (*A. gerardi*), broomsedge bluestem (*A. virginicus*), and splitbeard bluestem (*A. ternarius*).

Bulbous oat grass (*Arrhenatherum elatius bulbosum variegatum*)

Bulbous oat grass is a small, one-foot-tall, slow-growing but attractive grass for the spring and fall garden. Hailing from northern Europe, it is hardy in Zone 4. A cool-season grass, bulbous oat grass is also quite cold tolerant. Its white leaves are striped with a clear blue-green. Bulbous oat grass thrives on moisture and dislikes a dry situation. In climates with hot summers, bulbous oat grass may brown out in early summer, only to spring back as soon as cool weather returns. Even with this negative attribute, bulbous oat grass is worth growing as a fine white and blue-green striped ground cover or accent. It is particularly attractive with late spring bulbs and early perennials.

Giant reed (*Arundo donax*)

Arundo donax is a bold giant of a grass with bamboo-like canes that comes from southern Europe. A warm-season grass, it is hardy to Zone 6, and possibly to Zone 5 with winter protection. Excellent as a specimen or screen, it can reach fourteen feet or more in height. As is the case with many grasses, growth and ultimate size are dependent upon the amount of sun and moisture the grass receives, as well as soil and climatic conditions. Giant reed is a pastel-colored gray-green-blue and this, together with its size, makes it impossible to miss in the landscape. It is a colorful plant in a subtle, quiet way—its color is remarkable but tends to make the giant reed appear to recede. Broad, pointed leaves are held perpendicular to the stalks, which measure more than an inch in diameter. Leaves are opposite and held about six inches apart so that the canes have an open, lacy, bamboo-like appearance that doesn't make a very dense screen until the clump is very old or unless several plants are grouped together. Alternatively, it can be grouped with Eulalia grass or maiden grass for an excellent, almost impenetrable screen. Foot-long flowers are wonderful and excellent for arranging, but hard to appreciate outdoors, being carried on top of tall culms in late fall. In climates with very early frost, giant reed will not bloom.

If giant reed has a fault, it is that very often, in late summer, instead of standing absolutely erect, one side will sometimes fan out. Neatniks may wish to tie the grass back. Others may enjoy this irregularity. Giant reed has naturalized in South Carolina and farther south.

Arundo pliani, a very much smaller, wiry form of *Arundo*, has recently appeared on the market. Marginally hardy in Zone 7, it may prove to be a good alternative to the giant reed for small gardens.

Variegated giant reed *(Arundo donax variegata)*

Less hardy than the giant reed, variegated giant reed will survive in Zone 7. Similar to the giant reed in habit, it is smaller, growing only to about ten feet tall. Its leaves are striped green and cream. It is a stunning specimen.

Mosquito grass *(Bouteloua gracilis)*

Mosquito grass is an American native prairie grass that is hardy in Zone 4. A warm-season grass, it grows into a delicate, airy clump that withstands drought. In mid-summer, when curious flowers are borne on thin, wiry stems, the clump stands about two feet tall. Some people think the flowers look like mosquito larvae, others that they resemble a school of tiny fish. In any case, they are eye-catching. Mosquito grass works well in rock gardens or close to a path or patio, where its curious flowers can be seen close up. It can get along with very little irrigation and, for this reason, has been used with success as a water-saving lawn grass for dry climates. (Another water-saving lawn substitute is the creeping native buffalo grass, *Buchloe dactyloides*.)

Mosquito grass *(Bouteloua gracilis)* is a native prairie grass that withstands heat, drought, and extreme cold. Some think its curious flowers resemble mosquito larvae.

Quaking grass *(Briza media)*

Quaking grass grows into a ten-inch tuft of medium green. Hardy in Zone 4 and possibly Zone 3 with protection, quaking grass is native to Europe and Asia. It sends out short rhizomes and will self-sow, but neither of these characteristics is a problem. It is indifferent to many growing conditions and will perform equally well in a moist or dry spot and in light or heavy soils, although it does better in poor soils. Do not fertilize quaking grass! The glory of quaking grass and the source of its name is the panicle of wonderful, fat, pendulous, heart-shaped little flower heads dangling from delicate stems. These change over the summer from bright green to fleeting purple to a pale wheat color. They are excellent in dried arrangements. Quaking grass is also a good plant for the rock garden.

Feather reed grass *(Calamagrostis acutiflora stricta)*

Feather reed grass, a cool-season grass that is hardy in Zone 4, is the result of a cross between *Calamagrostis arundinacea* and *C. epigeios*. It is one of the few cool-season grasses that remains showy throughout the hottest days of summer—no matter how many of them there are. Completely revived from winter and nearly knee-high by the time the tulips bloom, feather reed grass grows quickly to four feet tall and produces lovely, airy, delicate white (later turning rose) twelve-inch-long flowers in June that are held above the plant. Everything about feather reed grass—its foliage, its flowers, its buff-colored seed heads that form in July—stands very upright and erect. For this reason, feather reed serves as an excellent vertical accent. It is useful for low screening, a stylized meadow planting, as a background plant, as a statuesque accent near a path, or rising out of low-growing ground cover. In fall, foliage turns lime-yellow before fading to yellow-tinged winter white. Feather reed grass is one of the best all-around grasses for use in the garden. It is trouble-free, not fussy about soil, withstands drought, and is quite hardy. Its upright habit, long season of flower, and fall and winter appearance make it a desirable and dependable ornamental. Although it will tolerate some shade, feather reed grass loses some of its starch and does not stand as erect in that situation.

Foxtail grass, or Korean feather reed *(Calamagrostis arundinacea brachytricha)*

Foxtail grass, hardy in Zone 5, grows to nearly three feet tall in full sun. Its medium green, narrow, pointed leaves angle out stiffly from the clump so that the grass suggests a pincushion or one of the

*Calamagrostis arundinacea
brachytricha*

narrow leaf forms of yucca. Its glory (and the reason people grow foxtail grass) is in the showy, big, pale lavender-white, twelve-inch-long, fluffy foxtail-shaped flowers that appear in fall. They are generously produced and held out pincushion-wise around the clump. Foxtail grass is a stunning specimen plant. Give it room to develop symmetrically. After frost, rain, hail, and sleet, foliage withers and plumes may become unattractive. Cut foxtail grass back at this time and wait for next fall.

Leatherleaf sedge, or New Zealand sedge (*Carex buchananii*)

The leatherleaf sedge, hardy in Zone 6, hails from New Zealand. It is renowned for its unusual army green/cinnamon brown color. Extremely fine, narrow leaves grow stiffly upright from the clump to about two feet and then taper at the ends, which curl under and twist into delicate spirals. Leatherleaf sedge, an evergreen, grows in moist sun or light shade. It is a beautiful plant but one that isn't easy to place in the garden because its subtle color gets lost. For more punch, use at least three plants and contrast with very dark green (mondo grass, *Deschampsia*) or yellow-greens (*Hosta* 'August Moon').

Carex conica marginata

Hardy in Zone 5, semi-evergreen *Carex conica marginata* is a sedge that grows only six inches tall and prefers a position in shade or semi-shade. It forms a delicate mound of deep green leaves that are finely striped white along the margins. Use *Carex conica marginata* as a fine, neat, low-growing ground cover in the shade.

Japanese silver sedge (*Carex morrowii variegata*)

Growing to about one foot tall in shade or part shade, Japanese silver sedge is an attractive accent or ground cover plant for dark places where fine white stripes along the margins of green leaves suggest flashes of silver. It is hardy in Zone 5. This semi-evergreen, once established, is much tougher than its appearance suggests, withstanding both heat and drought.

Variegated Japanese sedge (*Carex morrowii aureo-variegata*)

Variegated Japanese sedge grows to a bit more than one foot tall in shade or partial shade, and some people report good luck in full sun. Similar to the Japanese silver sedge in size and habit, variegated Japanese sedge is colored green and cream. Semi-evergreen, it is hardy in Zone 5 and makes a beautiful, colorful ground cover that lights up the dull places under trees.

Palm sedge (*Carex muskingumensis*)

Palm sedge, a feathery, delicate, bright, medium green shade-loving sedge, grows to about twenty inches tall. It makes an excellent ground cover under trees and can be used in small groups as a low, soft accent plant. The name "palm sedge" is suggested by its pattern of growth: eight-inch-long pointed leaves radiate from the tops of stiffly upright stems. Together they look a bit like parasols or palm fronds. Hardy in Zone 5, palm sedge may sulk in a very hot and dry summer. It revives quickly at the first sign of rain and cooler weather. Palm sedge is not evergreen. Struck by frost, it turns a delicate and fleeting shade of apricot before blanching to a bright almond color. Very attractive right after frost, it lacks the staying power of larger grasses. The wind soon shreds palm sedge. Cut it back when it ceases to please.

Black sedge (*Carex nigra*)

Black sedge, hardy in Zone 4, grows only six inches tall. It spreads to form dark blue-green tufts that serve as a neat, shade-tolerant ground cover. Black sedge, named for its black flower stalks, is useful in a rock garden or as a ground cover in shade or partial shade.

Bird's foot sedge (*Carex ornithopoda variegata*)

Bird's foot sedge is a delightful miniature, growing only four to six inches tall. Its creamy white leaves are striped dark green along the margins. It is hardy in Zone 7 and makes a superb rock garden plant for partial to full shade.

Drooping sedge, also called weeping sedge (*Carex pendula*)

Drooping sedge's thirty-inch, dark green, leathery leaves arise from a central tuft. Hardy in Zone 5, drooping sedge grows in moist shade, sending out long, dramatic flower stalks that, heavy with pendulous blooms, arch gracefully over the plant. Drooping sedge is a semi-evergreen cool-season plant that revives in very early spring. Its unique flowers appear in May and remain on the plant throughout the summer. It is not an easy plant to place because it is both dramatic and somewhat transparent in its effect. It needs a plain background so that its narrow graceful foliage and delicate arching flowers can be seen without distraction. Rocks or a low-growing, even-textured ground cover or a background of evergreens isolate it and set it off to advantage. Drooping sedge self-sows.

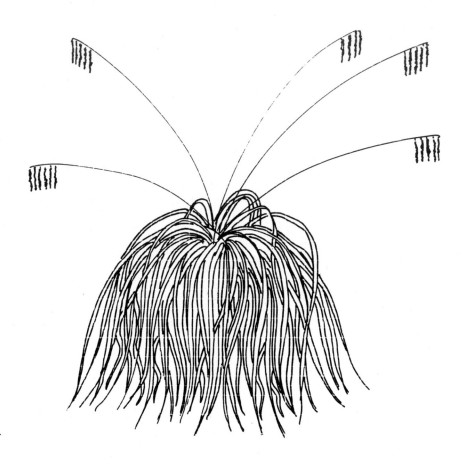

Carex pendula

Bowles Golden grass (*Carex stricta* 'Bowles Golden,' syn. *C. elata*)

Bowles Golden grass is a sedge that grows about twenty inches tall and is a clear golden yellow—the brightest yellow of any grass. It is absolutely stunning when paired with gold variegated hostas in gardens in half-shade. Bowles Golden grass is hardy in Zone 7.

Sea oats, also called northern sea oats, river oats (*Chasmanthium latifolium*, syn. *Uniola*)

An American native hardy in Zone 4, sea oats resembles a small, three-foot-tall bamboo with its rather light green leaves held perpendicularly and at four- to five-inch intervals on stiff, wire stems. When the inflorescence develops fully in late August, panicles droop under the weight of the pale green, flat, inverted, grainlike flowers. These are excellent for bouquets and arrangements. Sea oats is a warm-season clumping grass that increases very slowly from rhizomes. It grows best in a rich, humusy site in partial shade. It serves as an excellent tall ground cover, a transition plant between woodland and lawn, or an engaging specimen. Its inflorescence is desirable for flower arranging. Sea oats self-sows.

Pampas grass (*Cortaderia selloana*)

For a long time, pampas grass was the only ornamental grass most people knew about. It is a handsome, extremely dramatic grass, reaching twelve feet when its great puffy white flowers bloom. Clumps reach about five feet of dusty blue-green cascading foliage that is nearly as broad as it is tall before the spectacular flowers shoot up in fall to more than double the plant's size and impact. A warm-season grass, pampas grass comes from the pampas of Argentina. It requires both moist soil and good drainage, particularly in winter. Pampas grass serves as a riveting specimen and makes an excellent spot screen. Unfortunately, pampas grass is not reliably hardy outside of Zone 8. Some people report good results in colder zones when the plant is protected over winter with something like an overturned bushel basket or a bale of hay. To make sure that pampas grass doesn't freeze in zones where it is not hardy, plant it in a half-barrel and haul it in over the winter.

C. *selloana* 'Pumila' is a new, dwarf form of pampas grass that is reputedly hardier (Zone 7). It grows only about three feet tall with six-foot plumes.

Tufted hair grass (*Deschampsia caespitosa*)

Deep green tufted hair grass is a cool-season plant that grows to two feet. Very hardy (Zone 4), it is also evergreen. Tufted hair grass is native to many parts of the world and is usually found in moist, boggy places. It does best in a moist spot in partial shade and in cool summer climates. Tufted hair grass produces surprisingly delicate flowers in June that rise two feet above the plant and remain showy until winter winds shred them. Some cultivars with especially attractive tan to gold-colored infloresences are *Deschampsia caespitosa* 'Bronzeschleier (bronze haze) and *D. caespitosa* 'Goldgehaenge' (gold drops). Because their flowers are so fine and because tufted hair grass is grown primarily for its flowers, it needs careful placement as well as massing for best effect. A dark background like a yew or euonymus hedge or placement among rocks will enhance the impact of the flowers.

Lyme grass, or wild rye (*Elymus glaucus*)

Lyme grass is the bluest of all. Extremely hardy (in Zone 4), it is a dune grass from North America. In gardens it is grown for its

The great white plumes of pampas grass *(Cortaderia selloana)* are carried high above the clump.

144

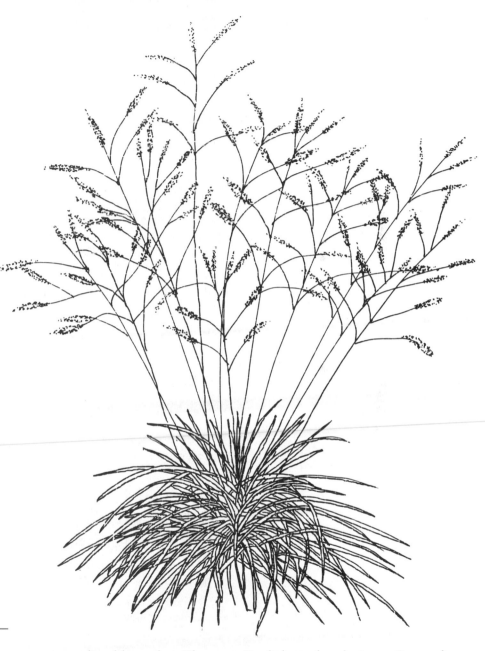

Deschampsia caespitosa

outstanding blue color. The great English garden designer Gertrude Jekyll grew the similar European native *Elymus arenarius* in her gray garden along with sea kale and tamarisk. This is a grass for a spot that bakes in the sun and gets buffeted by the wind. Lyme grass is an extremely tough plant that is also very aggressive, spreading quickly by stolons.

Ravenna grass *(Erianthus ravennae)*

Ravenna grass is sometimes called "northern pampas grass" because its habit is similar to that of *Cortaderia selloana*, but it is much hardier. It will survive, with winter protection, in the southern part of Zone 4. It is somewhat less symmetrical than pampas grass, but is similar in color, a gray-green. Early in the season, this warm-season grass is wider than it is tall. Toward fall, however, it seems to raise itself up as its incredibly long flower stalks develop. In an established clump of Ravenna grass, there can be as many as forty flower stalks shooting twelve to fourteen feet in the air in early fall. Ravenna grass responds to good light (full sun), soil fertility, and moisture (though it needs good drainage). To keep it under control, nurseryman Kurt Bluemel suggests "keeping it hungry." Ravenna grass serves as a dramatic specimen, a spot screen, or—when used with other grasses and shrubs—a privacy screen.

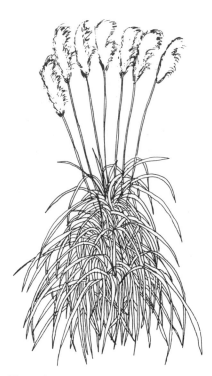

Erianthus ravennae

Rainbow fescue (*(Festuca amethystina* 'Superba')

Rainbow fescue is a true silvery blue, extremely hardy (in Zone 4) cool-season grass that blooms in late May and early June. Its flowers are lacy white and very upright and held about a foot over the eight-inch hummock of foliage. An excellent, neat, showy specimen throughout spring, rainbow fescue may brown out in a very long hot, dry summer.

April Green fescue (*Festuca cinerea* 'April Gruen')

April Green is a small, six-inch-tall, early and profusely blooming fescue. Extremely hardy in Zone 4, it is a cool-season grass that needs a position in full sun. When planted in masses, the blooms of April Green—which last for nearly a month—have a wonderful shimmering rainbow effect. Before bloom, April Green is a neat little, dusty green hummock. Afterward, if the weather is very hot and dry, April Green sulks or browns out. It begins to revive when the weather cools off. In a hot summer climate, give this plant camouflage during summer when it looks brown and disheveled.

Mueller's fescue (*Festuca muelleri*)

Mueller's fescue is green rather than blue and grows to about eight inches tall. It grows best in full sun and well-drained soil and, when grown in masses, makes an attractive, drought-tolerant, hummocky lawn substitute for difficult-to-mow or infrequently watered places. It is hardy in Zone 5.

Solling fescue (*Festuca ovina* 'Solling')

Solling is remarkable for two characteristics. A cool-season grass, it seldom blooms and therefore doesn't brown out after bloom, as many fescues do in hot summer climates. It remains a neat eight-inch hummock of powder blue foliage virtually year-round. It is hardy in Zone 5. Grow Solling in full sun with good drainage.

Dwarf bearskin fescue (*Festuca scoparia* 'Pic Carlit')

Tiny two-inch-tall dwarf bearskin fescue is a rock garden treasure. Hardy in Zone 4, it is an emerald green, cool-season, cool-temperature-loving grass for full sun or shade, where it does well, especially in Zone 7. Although it is very low-growing, it makes steady progress outward and soon covers a square foot or more with its brilliant green, mossy-looking foliage, which is prickly to the touch. In June, delicate flowers are borne about eight inches above the clump. These turn a contrasting golden tan color.

Hakonechloa macra

Not everybody succeeds with hakonechloa, but those who do love and treasure this plant. It is a very hardy (in Zone 4 with winter protection) cool-season grass that comes from the mountains of Japan. It grows to two feet and more when well established. Foliage is satiny soft to the touch, dark green, and falls in graceful layers to one side. It would seem that hakonechloa would be best suited to a cloud forest situation, yet there are excellent specimens in gardens around Washington, D.C., an area noted for its blazing, humid summers. Some people believe that it resents transplanting, others that it is sensitive to soil. It is so beautiful when established that it is worth any amount of trouble. Hakonechloa has been difficult to locate recently. If you can find it, buy it and try it. Give it the best: light shade and moist but draining soil that is deep and humusy.

Hakonechloa macra aureola

More striking than *H. macra,* especially because it brings light to a shady situation, variegated hakonechloa is a bright yellow-green variegated beauty that grows best in shade. Hardy in the southern part of Zone 4 with protection, it is a grass that blooms in August. Similar in habit and cultural requirements to *H. macra,* variegated hakonechloa is, however, more difficult to establish in a hot summer climate.

Side by side, two hakonechloas exhibit contrasting colors under the branches of a Harry Lauder's Walking Stick shrub at Brookside Gardens in Wheaton, Maryland. The variegated form, *Hakonechloa macra aureola*, is reputedly more difficult to grow in hot summer areas. (Brookside Gardens)

Helictotrichon sempervirens

Blue oat grass *(Helictotrichon sempervirens)*

Blue oat grass, a two-foot hedgehog-shaped true blue grass is an extremely hardy (in Zone 4) cool-season grass that blooms in May. Flowers are held on long, arching stems and are extremely showy. Blue when they appear, they turn a lovely, contrasting wheat color and bob over the plants, dancing in the wind. Blue oat grass needs full sun and good drainage.

Velvet grass *(Holcus lanatus variegatus)*

Velvet grass is one of the prettiest sights of the spring garden, reaching fresh perfection at tulip time. Its bright white and green striped, eight-inch-tall foliage serves as a stunning ground cover with early spring bulbs and white-flowering spring shrubs and trees. A cool-season grass that grows rapidly from rhizomes, it is hardy in Zone 4. In cool climates, velvet grass is a lovely ground cover that prefers sandy, well-drained soil. Anywhere that summers are hot, expect velvet grass to die down along with tulip foliage. In a climate with hot summers, treat it as a seasonal ornamental. Placement in shade may prolong its period of show.

Bottle brush grass *(Hystrix patula)*

Bottle brush grass is a lovely little woodland grass that grows in a ten-inch hummock of medium green. Hardy in Zone 5, it is a cool-season plant that needs good moisture in sun or a position in half-shade. Its name derives from the flower spikes, which resemble

Hystrix patula

light green bottle brushes. They appear in mid-summer and are held on long thirty-inch stems. These are good for flower arranging. Bottle brush is a quietly handsome grass. Unless planted en masse, it is easy to overlook. It serves as a graceful, natural-looking transition plant between woodland and lawn.

Japanese blood grass (*Imperata cylindrica* 'Red Baron')

Japanese blood grass is a relatively new import, but one we will see more and more frequently. It is valued for its unusual color. At the base of each clump, the grass blades are medium green. A few inches up each blade the color changes to red. At first it was thought that Japanese blood grass was extremely tender and needed a shady, sheltered position, but experience has borne out that it is hardy in Zone 5, and it is reported to survive in Zone 4 with protection. It does well in moist sun or half-shade and seems to color better with several hours of sun each day. Some people report excellent results with blood grass grown in full sun. Japanese blood grass spreads slowly by rhizomes to form small colonies whose color is most intense in late summer and fall. After hard frost, however, Japanese blood grass has no attraction. Gardeners are still learning how to use this twenty-inch-tall green and red grass. One thing is certain: One clump is not enough. Massing many plants together and a position where this stunning grass can be seen with light streaming through it greatly enhances its ornamental value.

Koeleria glauca

A colorful ground cover of ornamental grasses and perennials at the Brookside Gardens includes yellow-banded porcupine grass (*Miscanthus sinensis strictus,* left background), lavender *Perovskia* (right background), yellow false cypress, blue-gray juniper, and *Festuca,* and (in the foreground) day lilies, dwarf pine, and Japanese blood grass (*Imperata cylindrica* 'Red Baron'). (Brookside Gardens)

Silver hair grass (*Koeleria argentea*)

Silver hair grass grows in a striking one-foot, upright tuft of fine blue-silver foliage. Like many blue plants, it prefers full sun and a well-drained position in the garden in soil that is not too rich in nitrogen. It is a cool-season grass that is hardier than originally thought to be. Flowers are white and lacy, later forming yellow-tan seeds that contrast with the foliage.

Blue hair grass (*Koeleria glauca*)

Blue hair grass is similar to *K. argentea* but somewhat smaller and more hedgehog-like in appearance. It is a beautiful silver-blue. In Karl Foerster's groundbreaking book on grasses, *Einzug der Graeser in die Gaerten,* he suggested planting blue hair grass with junipers. It is an excellent suggestion. Not only does each member of the combination have the same cultural requirements, but their colors are compatible. In addition, when blue hair grass rests for a period after blooming, junipers carry on until cool weather returns and blue hair grass revives. Grow it in full sun with good drainage. Very hardy, there are reports from gardeners in zones 3 and 4 who grow it successfully. It is easy to start from seed.

151

Luzula pilosa

Snowy woodrush (*Luzula nivea*)

Ultimately larger (two feet tall) than either *L. pilosa* or *L. sylvatica*, the snowy woodrush takes longer to grow into its prime. Evergreen, shade-loving snowy woodrush bears showy fifteen-inch-long flowers in July or August that are useful in both fresh and dried arrangements. Snowy woodrush will grow into a splendid accent plant along a woodland path. German plantsman Karl Foerster suggested grouping it with ferns. Hardy in Zone 4, snowy woodrush thrives in acid soil. Like *L. pilosa* or *L. sylvatica*, it prefers moist, humusy soil but will tolerate dry shade.

Hairy woodrush (*Luzula pilosa*)

Very hardy (in Zone 3), the hairy woodrush is a low-growing, eight-inch-tall tufted rush that grows best in the shady, humusy soil of woodland or at the edge of woodland, where it makes rapid progress. The hairy woodrush, native to many parts of Europe, Siberia, and the Caucasus, is rhizomatous, producing the quickest cover where it is most at home. In a less-than-ideal spot, for example, in the dry shade under trees, it will still make steady progress once established. A cool-weather, evergreen grass, hairy woodrush is probably not a good plant for the very hot parts of the South, although it thrives in the Washington, D.C., area. Leaves are one-half inch wide, flat, shiny, tapering at the ends, and as tousled and tangled as loose ribbons. A bright yellow-green as it emerges from the clump, each blade, hairy along the edges, turns darker green toward the tip. Umbellate tan flowers appear in April on long stems. Hairy woodrush makes a fine evergreen ground cover in shade.

Greater woodrush (*Luzula sylvatica*)

Greater woodrush can reach nearly fifteen inches tall where it grows well. Similar in appearance to hairy woodrush, greater woodrush performs best in a woodland situation in shade, where it makes an evergreen, impenetrable ground cover, but like *L. pilosa*, it will also tolerate dry shade. It is reputedly less hardy than hairy woodrush (in Zone 5) but has the same tousled look. It, too, makes a tough ground cover around and among shrubs and shade-loving plants.

Spikey mellic (*Melica ciliata*)

When it is blooming, spikey mellic is a small treasure for the small garden. A cool-season grass, it blooms in the lull between the

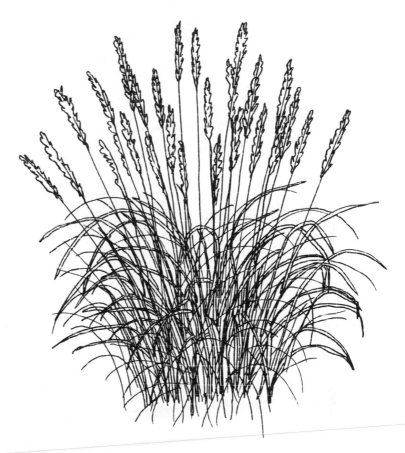

Melica ciliata

last of the bulbs and the first summer perennials. Spikey mellic grows to about eight inches of narrow-leaved blue-green hummock. In May, flowers form on fine, eighteen-inch stems and fan out over the plant. After bloom, the grass rests. For this reason, plant it where other low-growing ground cover plants will camouflage. Spikey mellic is hardy in Zone 5 and will tolerate some shade, particularly farther south.

Melica transylvanica

Hardy in Zone 5, M. *transylvanica* grows to about two feet of rather fine-leafed, clear green hummock. It is a cool-season grass that blooms in May, holding its long, narrow, light tan inflorescence on a two-foot stem. A small plant, use it in the rock garden or next to a tiny pool, where it will not overwhelm.

Golden grass (Milium effusum aureum)

Sometimes mistakenly called "Bowles Golden," golden grass is not really golden, but a bright yellow-green, extremely showy,

A bold group of purple coneflower (*Echinacea purpurea*) combines well with giant miscanthus (*Miscanthus floridulus*), often bare below the knees.

154

The inflorescence of Eulalia grass
(*Miscanthus sinensis*) unfolds rose-
colored and satiny.

155

shade- and moisture-loving cool-season millet. It grows to about fifteen inches tall, spreading slowly by rhizomes. It prefers cool weather and may die out over the summer or completely in hot summer climates. Where it can be grown successfully, however, it is a stunning subject for massing. The yellow-green color is riveting—a definite brightener for a dull shady spot. Golden grass is hardy in Zone 6 and can be grown from seed.

Giant miscanthus (Miscanthus floridulus, syn. M. sinensis giganticus, M. japonicus)

Giant miscanthus, a warm-season grass, grows to ten feet tall. Its broad, one-inch wide, white mid-ribbed leaves taper to fine points. Growing upward along the very upright canes, they arch over as they grow long. Layers of arching leaves suggest cascading water. Giant miscanthus is a bold specimen grass—all by itself in the middle of a lawn, next to a path or driveway, or among low-growing ground cover plants. It also makes a good screen. Wherever it is hardy (Zone 6), giant miscanthus proves an easy-to-grow, undemanding plant. It tolerates shade, root competition, full sun, and a somewhat dry position. With rich, moist but well-draining soil, giant miscanthus will outdo itself and grow taller and wider in less time.

Silver banner grass (Miscanthus sacchariflorus)

Very hardy (into Zone 4), this five-foot-tall October-blooming grass is aggressive and not recommended for small gardens. Buyer beware! Sometimes it is sold by the unscrupulous to the unwary as pampas grass or Eulalia grass. It never forms the handsome clumps of either of those grasses, but retains an upright habit, similar to that of giant miscanthus (M. floridulus), and it spreads quickly. It is useful on the edge of ponds in wild gardens.

Eulalia grass (Miscanthus sinensis)

Miscanthus sinensis is the species from which some of the most beautiful and useful ornamental grasses have been selected. Long grown in China and Japan, the Victorians embraced Eulalia grass. Growing six to seven feet tall, it serves as a splendid specimen or a dense hedge. It is a warm-season grass, hardy in Zone 4. It prefers full sun but will tolerate a bit of shade, although in this situation it sometimes droops or lists to one side. Eulalia grass needs room. Give it at least five feet in diameter. Frost blanches Eulalia grass to a pale almond color that is particularly handsome when contrasted with evergreens.

Miscanthus sinensis condensatus

Condensatus is a handsome, robustly growing variety of Eulalia grass that is somewhat bolder in habit. Hardy in Zone 4, condensatus blooms early, making it an excellent choice for climates with short falls and early frosts. Pale gold, fan-shaped flowers emerge in August or early September, later turning to magenta. They are held about two feet above the broad five-foot-tall clump. Give condensatus full sun. In partial shade, the clump is dwarfed and flowering is delayed. After frost, condensatus turns buff and is attractive throughout the winter. There is a very attractive variegated cultivar, 'Silberpfeil,' that seems a bit less likely to droop than *M. sinensis variegatus.*

Maiden grass (*Miscanthus sinensis* 'Gracillimus')

Maiden grass, with its long, arching, fine foliage, is the most formal and most elegant of the big miscanthus grasses. Blades, seven feet long with a white mid-vein, are only a quarter inch wide. They rise erectly from the base of the grass and curve into an elegant vase shape. Of all of the forms of miscanthus, maiden grass is the most suitable for a formal garden because of its fine texture and symmetrical shape. Flowers—white and fan-shaped—rise over the clump in October. With repeated frosts, maiden grass slowly turns color. Vivid, sparkling summer green becomes dull and seems to bleed away. In winter, the clump is the color of dried corn husks.

'Morning Light' miscanthus (*Miscanthus sinensis* 'Morning Light')

'Morning Light' is a delicate new variegated miscanthus first offered by Kurt Bluemel Nurseries. Hardy in Zone 5, 'Morning Light' is a small warm-season grass that blooms in fall. Smaller than the species, 'Morning Light' reaches only four feet of clump. Because its blades are quite fine, its variegation presents not as distinctly clear green and white stripes, but as a pale, almost ghostly blending of these colors. The sum of its fine variegation is a wondrously delicate, subtle new color: a fine, pastel gray-green that is especially handsome with glaucous plants and other pastels.

Flame grass (*Miscanthus sinensis purpurascens*)

A warm-season grass for a position in full sun, flame grass is extremely hardy (into Zone 4). It grows to about fifty inches tall, sending up satiny, magenta-colored fans in late summer. Later these turn a bright silken white. Early flowering makes flame grass an

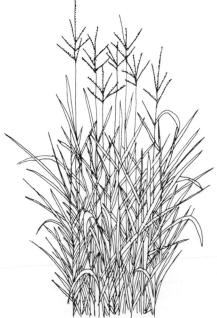

Miscanthus sinensis purpurascens

excellent choice for climates with early frosts, where later-blooming flowers on grasses such as M. *sinensis* 'Gracillimus' may not have long enough to develop before frost. A clump of flame grass slowly adds girth so that a ten-year-old specimen may be thirty inches across or more. Leaves are three-quarters of an inch wide and so upright in habit that this grass exhibits a strong vertical character. Even when closely spaced as a ground cover, clumps of flame grass do not merge together but retain their individual upright look. In fall, leaves begin to color bright red-orange. When viewed with light streaming through the red foliage from behind the grass, it appears to be in flames. Wonderful anywhere, flame grass is outstanding as a specimen for a small townhouse or dooryard garden, where its striking fall and winter coloring—especially when contrasted with dark evergreens—will be an attractive focus that is not overpowering. The deep blue-green of hollies or cotoneaster is the perfect complement to flame grass's red-orange.

Silver feather grass (*Miscanthus sinensis* 'Silberfeder')

Elegant silver feather grass, introduced in 1967 by Dr. Hans Simon, is a thoroughly satisfactory grass. It is so similar in size, habit, and hardiness to the species, that it is difficult to say exactly why it is a bit more refined, a bit more graceful, a bit more elegant than M. *sinensis*. Certainly, its shimmering white fan-shaped blooms, emerging as early as August, are an advantage—especially in cold climates, where very late flowering grasses are nipped in the bud. Silver feather is hardy in Zone 5 and may be hardy in Zone 4 with protection.

Variegated miscanthus (*Miscanthus sinensis variegatus*)

Clean, distinct green and white stripes set variegated miscanthus apart wherever and however it is planted. Stunning as a specimen in a container or rising out of low ground cover against a dark background, variegated miscanthus also works well in a garden border, where its colors complement pastels and white-flowering plants. Hardy in Zone 6, variegated miscanthus is a warm-season grass that grows somewhat less lustily than other miscanthus. Give it a position in sun or (in the South) partial shade.

Porcupine grass (*Miscanthus sinensis strictus*)

Both porcupine grass and zebra grass (M. *sinensis zebrinus*) are a bright green with yellow horizontal bands on their six-foot-long blades. Both are warm-season grasses that grow in full sun, but there the likeness ends. While porcupine grass stands strictly upright, forming a very neat, well-shaped clump that only fans out in

October, fast-growing zebra grass always seems to fall open in the middle, sprawling over its neighbors. Plant porcupine grass for a very upright, almost rigid accent.

Moor grass (*Molinia caerulea arundinacea* 'Windspiel')

One of the most exciting grasses, moor grass is a dancing grass. Its delicate, wire-fine yellow seed heads on stiff, seven-foot stems are set into slow motion by the breeze. Flowers appear in mid-summer and are held above the two-foot, green clumps for four months or more. Moor grass needs space and sensitive placement for best results. Because the stems are long and thin, they are transparent and look best when located against a plain background. Because the stems arch far over the plant, give it a four- or five-foot berth and banish tall neighbors. *Molinia caerulea arundinacea* 'Transparent' is a slightly smaller plant with shorter flower spikes. Low-growing, two-foot-tall *Molinia caerulea arundinacea* serves as an excellent ground cover plant. All three forms are hardy in Zone 4. All tolerate light shade in the South.

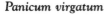

Panicum virgatum

Switch grass *(Panicum virgatum)*

North American native switch grass is a warm-season prairie grass that may grow to six feet tall but more commonly grows to about four feet. It is anchored by roots twice as deep as the grass is high. It withstands drought and high temperatures but also survives extreme cold. Drought conditions will miniaturize switch grass. It is hardy in Zone 3. A sod-forming grass, switch grass quickly develops into a bushy subject in the garden. Clouds of white float over the green, airy grass in mid-summer, when it blooms. Often, especially when there is no neighbor plant for support, switch grass will bend or even flop over. After frost, however, the entire plant stiffens and turns a warm, glowing wheat color that is effective all winter long. When grown en masse, switch grass is the best choice for winter show. Cut it back in early spring.

Red switch grass *(Panicum virgatum* 'Haense Herms,' *P. virgatum* 'Rotstrahlbusch,' *P. virgatum* 'Rehbraun')

Only three to four feet tall, these shorter cultivars of switch grass are generally more upright than the species. In addition, red-colored seeds and outstanding red fall coloring add to their garden interest.

Panicum virgatum 'Strictum'

Shorter and more upright than ordinary switch grass, *P. virgatum strictum* has a slightly glaucous blue leaf. It reaches five feet high when it blooms and is as hardy as *P. virgatum* (into Zone 3), and as striking in winter.

Fountain grass *(Pennisetum alopecuroides)*

Fountain grass is hardy in Zone 6, but many gardeners have had success with it in Zone 5, and there are reports that it survives with protection in the southern part of Zone 4. Plant fountain grass in full sun in the North. In the South, it will tolerate light shade. It is a warm-season grass, emerging at tulip time to form dense but very graceful clumps of cascading foliage up to thirty-six inches tall. It is attractive from June, when it has achieved its characteristic habit, until February or March, when it needs cutting back.

In late summer, fountain grass is covered with fresh buff-colored flower heads—about six inches long—with a pink, maroon, or magenta cast (caused by maroon-colored awns that appear later). Flowers are held close to the clump and share the same cascading habit as the foliage. These flowers are particularly lovely in the

Pennisetum alopecuroides

mornings, when they shimmer with dew. Seed heads remain on the plant far into winter.

In fall, when fountain grass begins to fade very slowly into winter, it still retains much of its volume and thus keeps the garden from looking as bleak and empty as it might. Foliage may color briefly in shades of rose, apricot, or gold before turning the characteristic bright almond color that is extremely showy throughout winter.

Fountain grass is the best grass for all-around garden use. Planted at thirty- to thirty-six-inch intervals or closer, it is perfect as a meadow-like ground cover. One look and people conclude that this is its ideal use. Yet it is equally appropriate and attractive in Victorian pattern gardens or traditional flower borders. Used singly as an accent next to a path or in softening a corner of paving, it adds an utterly fitting, beautiful note of grace.

Dwarf fountain grass (*Pennisetum alopecuroides* 'Hameln')

This dwarf form of *P. alopecuroides* grows only about twenty-four inches tall and is in every way a smaller, more compact version of the straight species.

Black-seeded fountain grass (*Pennisetum alopecuroides* 'Moudry,' *Pennisetum alopecuroides viridescens*)

Smaller than *P. alopecuroides* and blooming later, the black-seeded fountain grasses bear long inflorescences, cast black by dark-

Pennisetum caudatum

colored awns. Black-seeded fountain grasses are hardy in Zone 7. Plant in full sun.

White-flowered fountain grass (*Pennisetum caudatum*)

This white-flowered pennisetum grows up to five feet when in bloom in very rich, moist soil. Elsewhere the clump grows to thirty inches. It is similar in appearance to *P. alopecuroides* but bears its large white flowers on long stems held about one foot above the clump. It is a graceful plant that is extremely showy in autumn. It is hardy in Zone 5.

Pennisetum incomptum (syn. *flaccidum*)

Pennisetum incomptum—sometimes called running fountain grass—doesn't resemble a fountain at all. It is a thin, upright, open-looking grass with aggressive runners that serves as a fast-growing ground cover. It grows to four feet. Hardy in Zone 6 (and probably Zone 5), it is a warm-season grass that blooms in mid-summer. Flowers are four to five inches long and about three-eighths of an inch wide.

Orient fountain grass (*Pennisetum orientale*)

Orient fountain grass, hardy in Zone 7, is smaller than *P. alopecuroides,* growing only about thirty inches tall with foliage that is slightly gray-green. Its pink flowers appear in early summer and have a cottony appearance. Plant Orient fountain grass in full sun.

Ribbon grass, or gardener's garters (*Phalaris arundinacea picta*)

Strongly rhizomatous, ribbon grass grows to three feet tall, quickly forming a bright, lively-looking, semi-evergreen ground cover in almost any soil, wet or dry. Clay soil and less-than-optimum conditions (drought, shade) may slow it down a bit. Very hardy in Zone 4 (with reports of success in Zone 3), ribbon grass is a striking, all-season ground cover plant that is also suitable for containers. In summer, it produces rather inconspicuous flowers. Norm Hooven, of the Limerock Ornamental Grass Nursery, suggests mowing ribbon grass down when it becomes coarse or tired-looking for fresh, new foliage.

Common reed (*Phragmites australis*)

The common reed grows almost everywhere on earth (hardy in Zone 4, but probably also Zone 3). It is usually found growing in full sun and standing water or on the edge of a marsh or pond, where it will reach nineteen feet high. It will also grow in moist garden situations where a very tall grass is needed. Wherever the common reed grows, expect to see birds who enjoy its shelter. *Phragmites australis aurea*, a gold and green variegated dwarf form that is about two feet tall, may soon be available from grass nurseries.

Autumn moor grass *(Sesleria autumnalis)*

Bright green with a yellow cast, autumn moor grass grows into a spikey, one-foot-tall clump of stiff, narrow blades. In spite of its small stature, autumn moor grass is a sculptural plant. In early fall, a narrow, two-and-a-half-inch, silvery white inflorescence forms and contrasts with foliage. Autumn moor grass is hardy in Zone 5 and will grow in full sun or partial shade. It makes an excellent hummocky ground cover or addition to a rock garden.

Indian grass **(*Sorghastrum nutans*, syn. *Chrysopogon nutans*)**

As its name suggests, Indian grass is a North American native. It is extremely hardy (probably into Zone 3). Grass expert Mary Hockenberry Meyer names Indian grass along with other warm-

Sorghastrum nutans

Rich bamboo-like texture and showy flowers adorn *Spodiopogon sibiricus,* growing in artist Bob Dash's Long Island garden. Flowers of the spodiopogon and, at right, the *Molinia caerulea arundinacea* 'Windspiel' show off to advantage against a dark background. (Design: Bob Dash)

season prairie grasses as "true champions of adverse conditions." Able to survive intensely cold winters and very hot summers, Indian grass is also an attractive ornamental for massing or for use as a specimen. It forms bunches and patches of sod that reach four feet with pointed one-third-inch-wide gray-green blades that stand fairly erect in the center of a clump but arch over around the edges. In late August/early September, flowers open—shiny, lacy, eight inches long, and rusty rose, later forming plumes of harvest gold. They are held about thirty inches above the foliage. Later, tiny yellow anthers dangle from the flowers.

Prairie cord grass (*Spartina pectinata aureo-marginata*)

A tough North American prairie grass, cord grass withstands extremes of temperature. It is hardy in Zone 3 and comes unscathed through the hottest, driest summer. A sod-forming, warm-season grass, prairie cord grass has long blades—up to thirty inches—that double over. Delicate yellow stripes run along the finely toothed leaf margins. Prairie cord grass is not fussy about soil conditions, growing in sandy or heavy and dry or wet soils. In fall, it colors gloriously yellow, retaining a yellowish cast into winter. Although it will tolerate some shade, cord grass stands more erect in full sun.

Spodiopogon sibiricus (syn. *Achnatherum, Muehlenbergia*)

Spodiopogon grows to a stiffly held five feet tall with short, pointed leaves held out perpendicular to the stems, giving the grass strong horizontal lines. Very hardy (in Zone 4), this cool-season grass prefers light shade and moist but well-drained soil. Like a piece of sculpture with complex form, spodiopogon serves as an excellent specimen. Its clean attractive foliage gives it the appearance of a bushy, fan-shaped clumping bamboo. In July, very showy, airy flowers form, and these remain on the plant until October. With frost, spodiopogon turns quickly from green to brown. Cut it down when foliage withers.

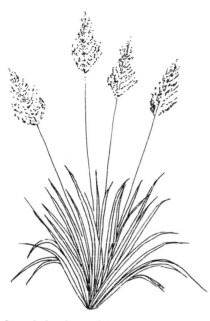

Sporobolus heterolepsis

Prairie dropseed (*Sporobolus heterolepsis*)

Growing to twenty inches tall, prairie dropseed, the hands-down favorite of native grass growers, is a warm-season grass that blooms in July. Inflorescence is a showy and delicate eight-inch panicle. Clump-forming and hardy in Zone 4 (possibly in Zone 3), prairie dropseed is gold-colored in the fall and blanches to cream in winter.

Giant feather grass (*Stipa gigantea*)

A cool-season grass from the mountains of Spain, giant feather grass is an unforgettable specimen in bloom. Giant feather grass grows to a two-foot hummock of gray-green foliage that prefers sun and a well-drained situation. In June, five-foot-tall flower spikes support great, billowy, eighteen-inch-long panicles of flowers that remain on the plant until August. Hardy in Zone 7, the very best climate for giant feather grass is a temperate one where temperatures are neither too hot nor too cold. In very hot summer climates, giant feather grass may brown out. It is so attractive, however, that it is worth a try and a good deal of trouble.

Stipa gigantea

9. ANNUAL GRASSES

ALL OF THE ANNUAL GRASSES listed below can be started from seed. You can harvest your own seed each summer for planting the following spring. These grasses do best in full sun, and all are useful both for fresh and dried arrangements.

Cloud grass *(Agrostis nebulosa)*

Easily started from seed, cloud grass grows to eighteen inches tall. It derives its name from clusters of small white flower spikes borne on stems about one foot high. Alternatively, these cloudy flower heads, most effective when grouped together, serve to hide the leggy, angular stems of other flowers in the garden.

Large quaking grass *(Briza maxima)*

Large quaking grass grows from seed started outdoors in the early spring. It grows to about eighteen inches tall and bears one- to two-inch-long oatlike seed heads on fine drooping stems.

Small quaking grass *(Briza minor)*

Small quaking grass is a miniature form of its large relative, bearing tiny, nearly heart-shaped, one-eighth-inch-long seed heads on delicate, arching stems.

ABOVE: The flowers of annual *Pennisetum setaceum*

166

Job's tears *(Coix lacryma-Jobi)*

Long known in gardens as an ornamental grass, Job's tears is grown primarily for its hard seeds, which may be white, gray, or black. Foliage usually grows to about three or four feet but may reach six feet in height. Soak seeds overnight or longer before starting them indoors.

Squirrel tail grass *(Hordeum jubatum)*

Squirrel tail grass grows to about eighteen inches tall and bears pale, fluffy seed heads three inches long and colored green to beige. Sow seeds outside as soon as the ground can be worked.

Job's tears *(Coix lacryma-Jobi)* has been grown in gardens since the Middle Ages, when its hard seeds were used for rosary beads.

Clumps of pink-flowered annual fountain grass *(Pennisetum setaceum)* soften the paving in Jack Chandler's Napa Valley garden. (Design: Jack Chandler)

The fat, fluffy flowers of annual feathertop *(Pennisetum villosum)* bloom in concert with summer flowers at the Park Seed Company's demonstration garden in Greenwood, South Carolina.

Rabbit tail grass (*Lagarus ovatus*)

Rabbit tail grass grows about eighteen inches tall and bears two-inch-long pale beige tufts of seeds. Sow seeds directly into the garden in early spring.

Pink, purple, and red fountain grasses (*Pennisetum setaceum, P. setaceum* 'Atrosanguineum,' *P. setaceum* 'Cupreum,' *P. setaceum* 'Rubrum')

Except for its pink-colored flowers, *Pennisetum setaceum*, an annual in the North, is in habit and size very similar to the perennial *Pennisetum alopecuroides*. However, its cultivars, handsome plants with broader leaves and a more upright habit, do not resemble *P. setaceum*. 'Atrosanguineum' has an upright habit with much broader, deep maroon-colored leaves and long purple flowers. 'Cupreum' has red foliage and copper flowers. 'Rubrum' has rather rosy red broad blades and rose-colored flowers.

Feathertop (*Pennisetum villosum*)

Exceptionally easy to start from seed started inside or planted outside when the ground has warmed, feathertop grows to about two feet tall and bears dozens of fat, fluffy, creamy white flowers four to five inches long.

10. BAMBOO

ABOVE: The leaves of *Sasa veitchii*

BAMBOO BELONGS to a subgroup of the grass family that is widely grown in the Orient, where it is admired for its beauty and harvested for food and timber. In the United States, it is better known as an ornamental than as a food and timber-producing plant.

"This plant is under-rated in the United States," says Richard Waters, of A Bamboo Shoot Nursery in Sebastopol, California. "Bamboos are beautiful evergreens whose new shoots are edible. The uses for the mature culms are endless."

There are 1200 species of bamboo, most of which grow in the tropics. People living in Florida, along the Gulf Coast, and in southern California can choose from among many beautiful species. The farther north a gardener lives, however, the fewer the choices.

There are clumping as well as running bamboos. Unfortunately, all but a few species of the clumping type are very tender, requiring temperatures that do not fall below 15° Fahrenheit. Many people regard the running types with uneasiness if not outright fear. One hears stories of lawsuits by neighbors whose yards were taken over by bamboo from the next property, or of bamboo coming up through asphalt.

"The golden bamboo (*Phyllostachys aurea*) gives the rest of the family a bad name," says Gib Cooper, of Tradewinds Bamboo

Nursery in Calpella, California. Golden bamboo is an aggressive running bamboo. A better choice is a clumping bamboo that does not run and requires less maintenance. If you want the look of a grove rather than of a clump, choose a running bamboo that is not aggressive and contain it.

HOW TO GROW BAMBOO

Steve Ray has grown bamboo for twenty-five years and "never gets tired of looking at it." Over the years, he has observed its growth closely. "Bamboo," he says, "is almost pest-free, evergreen [changes leaves once a year], needs very little care, and has a serene quality no other plant has." He recommends the following for growing healthy bamboo:

Soil and Terrain

"Bamboo thrives in fertile, well-drained soil, rich in organic material that is neutral or almost neutral in pH—soil that would grow a good crop of corn. For the best growth, an acid soil should be neutralized. Agricultural lime is ideal. . . . Bamboo also grows fairly well in poor soil [but] will not survive if planted in a boggy, marshy place. A gentle, sloping, sunny hillside shielded from the bitter north wind is a good location for planting. Bamboo grown in a sheltered location can survive lower temperatures than bamboo planted in an open location. In extremely cold areas, a heavy mulch will protect the roots, but the plant may become deciduous and all top growth may be killed each winter [and the plant] will not reach its maximum size. The roots usually survive to sprout the following spring. By using these precautions and allowing for winter kill of the top growth, bamboos can be grown far north of their normal range of hardiness."

Light

"Most bamboos do best in full or nearly full sunlight. All members of the *Phyllostachys* and *Arundinaria* [genera] grow well in the sun, with maybe a touch of shade to shield them from the blazing afternoon sun. Most of the little sasas grow well in semi-shade. Bamboo planted in the wrong light situation will not grow well."

Planting

"For best results dig up an area at least four feet square. Work [in] any rotted organic material such as leaf mold, compost, and manure that is available. Sand and peat moss are also good soil additives. A half cup of lime should be sufficient for the average application in the average planting. Churn together, water, firm the ground, and water again well. Water again several times shortly thereafter. In a very dry location, such as on a hill, plant the bamboo in a slight depression to trap and hold water."

Mulch

"Bamboo loves mulch such as leaves, grass clippings, pine straw, compost. The use of mulch helps conserve moisture, cuts down on weeding chores, and adds organic materials and trace elements to the soil. On new planting, the mulch layer should be light, probably two or three inches. Later the bamboo can be mulched to depths of six inches or more."

Moisture

"Bamboo should not be allowed to dry out too much the first year until it becomes established. During long dry spells, bamboo can be watered some every day."

Cultivation and Weeding

"Rhizomes grow close to the surface and may be damaged by deep cultivation. The use of a mulch is much better for weed control on a new planting. *Do not use weed killers around bamboo. Make sure the fertilizers do not have weed killers in them.*"

Pruning

"Keep any dead culms cut out of your bamboo."

Fertilizing Bamboo

Richard Waters, whose A Bamboo Shoot Nursery specializes in rare and unusual varieties of clumping and running bamboos, says, "Bamboos are sodium- and chlorine-sensitive and show leaf burn if these are present in the water or fertilizers. For this reason, do not use ocean-derived fertilizers in succession. Composted horse manure, cottonseed meal, and blood meal are all good for optimum growth."

Hardiness

Like grasses, bamboos are probably much hardier than the ratings given to them. Wayne Winterrowd, who grows bamboo at North Hill, a garden-design company, in Readsboro, Vermont,

Canes of the golden bamboo *(Phyllostachys aurea)* rise above a ground cover of ivy, Virginia creeper, and ostrich fern in Jack Lenor Larsen's Long Island garden. (Design: Jack Lenor Larsen)

Phyllostachys and ivy mingle on both sides of a narrow path to Jack Lenor Larsen's "Roundhouse" on Long Island. Mr. Larsen feels that people are needlessly afraid of bamboo, which, he says, is contained by cutting back yearly during its shooting period. (Design: Jack Lenor Larsen)

thinks they are "definitely worth a try farther north. You have to make a distinction between top hardiness [the survival of the old leaves and culms over winter] and root hardiness [the survival of the roots]. I think I'm right in saying that catalogs tend to list top hardiness." He adds that he grows a dozen or so from which he removes the tatty and winter-killed top growth each spring. Fresh new leaves form quickly thereafter. Mr. Winterrowd also credits "careful siting" and winter cover as important cultural practices in the North. Plants whose top growth he wishes to retain, he bends to the ground and covers with evergreen boughs. Among the bamboos Mr. Winterrowd and his partner, Joe Eck, grow at North Hill are *Arundinaria viridi-striata, Phyllostachys aureosulcata, Sinarundinaria nitida,* and *Thamnocalamus spathaceus.*

How to Curb Runners

It is true that a rampantly running bamboo, when neglected and not properly curbed, will do some of the terrible things people say it will do. However, containing bamboo is easily accomplished through barriers and by cutting back new shoots. In temperate climates, bamboo has a distinct period of shooting, usually in late spring. If it is cut back at this time, new shoots will not grow into culms (stalks). Steve Ray, of Steve Ray's Bamboo Gardens in Birmingham, Alabama, says that when he sees a shoot coming up where he doesn't want it, he simply kicks it over. "I can kick faster than it can grow," he says.

Underground containment in concrete pipes, flue tiles, or metal sheeting will curb runners. Mowing restrains bamboo that is planted in the middle of a lawn.

Gerald Bol, of Bamboo Sourcery, a bamboo nursery in Sebastopol, California, recommends these curbing methods of runners:

□ *Restrict water to where you wish the plant to grow.* This works best in a dry climate. Rhizomes steer toward moisture. If you can keep the surrounding areas dry, rhizomes should stay within the desired area.

□ *Kick over the brittle young shoots when they first appear.* After a while they should stop coming up. In temperate climates, most bamboos shoot in the spring, so vigilance is only required for a month or so. Many so-called running bamboos are not particularly aggressive. They mostly stay in a clump with but a few rhizomes wandering out. (Look for these in catalogs and/or ask your nurseryman.)

□ *Install a barrier in the ground.* Use concrete, 60-millimeter plastic, or some other impervious permanent substance. For species that get forty feet or more tall, make the barrier three feet deep. For others, two feet should be enough.

☐ *Dig a ditch.* Rhizomes will surface on the sides of the ditch and can then easily be removed. The depth should be comparable to the dimensions suggested for the barrier.

☐ *Put water in the ditch.* Most species do not like water-logged soil and will not willingly penetrate it. In this case, the ditch need not be deep.

☐ *Turn chickens loose.* They love the new shoots and will eat any that come up.

☐ *Plant a sun-loving species in the shade.* It will grow very slowly but probably will still look okay and will run little if at all.

☐ *Keep plants in containers.* The problems with this are that containers are a little harder to keep watered, and plants don't grow as big.

Use good judgment. With regard to using running bamboos, Steve Ray, of Bamboo Gardens in Birmingham, Alabama, adds, "Don't put one in the middle of your best day lily bed." He points out that there are many situations in which bamboo's spreading characteristic works to the gardener's advantage. Privacy screens, woodland ground covers, and steep banks are but a few.

Growing Bamboo in Containers

Robert L. Perry, of Sunset Nursery, Inc., in Tampa, Florida, suggests another way for gardeners to enjoy bamboo that is not cold hardy enough for their region: "Many of the 'tropical' bamboos are shunned because of the low temperature tolerance, which creates injury," says Mr. Perry, but this is not a problem when bamboo is used as an indoor plant.

"Bamboo is one of the most forgiving of plants that can be used in the home," says Mr. Perry. "After some thirty-eight years as a nurseryman, I have not seen any plant take as much abuse as bamboo and come right back up." He recommends "good potting soil, attention to watering [moist, not wet], and liquid fertilizer on a regular basis." Place the plant "near a window with filtered light." (Indoor gardeners living north of Florida may have to provide the bamboo with the brightest available light.) "Strong artificial light is also acceptable." He suggests "a container with sloping sides. In time the bamboo gets potbound . . . if you have a running type, there will be an abundance of rhizomes wound around [inside] the pot. These can be easily removed. . . . If you have a 'clumper' it will need some of the excess cut away." When this necessary thinning is done, he says, "repot the original plant with fresh soil and fertilizer cubes."

RECOMMENDED VARIETIES

Of the hundreds of beautiful bamboos currently available, a few stand out for landscape use because of their pattern of growth and their hardiness. For gardeners concerned about bamboo's tendency to send out runners, a clumping bamboo is the answer.

"If your lowest temperature does not fall below 15 degrees Fahrenheit, I highly recommend the genus *Bambusa*, which contains a wide variety of species—all of which are clumping," says Richard Waters. "If your temperature does fall below 15 degrees Fahrenheit, I recommend *Sinarundinaria nitida*, a shade-loving clumping bamboo that is hardy to minus 20 degrees Fahrenheit."

For gardeners concerned about the winter kill of top growth, *Phyllostachys*, one of the hardiest species, is the answer.

Todd Mumma, of the American Bamboo Company of Dayton, Ohio, reports that his nursery specializes in *Phyllostachys* varieties that are "hardy and field grown in Ohio . . . since 1956." American Bamboo Company grows twenty-five varieties. Mr. Mumma recommends planting "only when rhizomes are dormant in late winter or early spring." In addition, plants require "good drainage, plenty of water, and [they] must be mulched in winter in northern areas."

The following list contains only a few species, chosen for their good looks, clumping habit, exceptional hardiness, drought tolerance, or a combination of outstanding characteristics.

Arundinaria viridi-striata

Arundinaria viridi-striata is an attractive, variegated yellow and green, low-growing running bamboo that reaches only about eighteen to twenty-four inches. If heavily mulched, it will withstand temperatures of $-20°$ F and does better in a cooler climate. Where summers are hot, it grows best in shade.

Chinese Goddess bamboo (*Bambusa glaucescens riviereorum*, syn. *Bambusa multiplex*)

Chinese Goddess bamboo grows to only about six feet tall. Fussy about soil, it is, nevertheless, worth a try, especially as a bonsai subject. A clumping bamboo with small leaves on delicate branches, it is also beautiful in any garden where it can be grown. It is hardy to about 17° F and tolerates some shade.

Mexican weeping bamboo (*Otatea acuminata aztecorum*)

Mexican weeping bamboo withstands dry conditions and temperatures to 15° F. A clumper, it is found growing among stands of chaparral. It grows to twenty feet fall.

A low-growing bamboo, *Arundinaria viridi-striata*, confined by a sunken planter (right foreground) grows in concert at the Brookside Botanic Gardens with evergreens, perennials, and ornamental grasses. *Alopecurus pratensis aureus* grows in small clumps to the left. The grass directly behind the *Arundinaria* is feather reed grass (*Calamagrostis acutiflora stricta*) in seed. (Design: Hans Hanses)

Golden groove bamboo (*Phyllostachys aureosulcata*)

Golden groove bamboo is a running bamboo, hardy to 0° F and probably root hardy to −20° F. Culms are grooved and sometimes grow with occasional zigzags to about twenty feet. Leaves are a clean, bright yellow-green. Its shoots are good for eating.

David Bisset bamboo (*Phyllostachys bissetii*)

David Bisset bamboo is one of the hardiest bamboos. A runner, it grows to twenty feet tall with culms that are one inch in diameter and bear dark green leaves.

Black bamboo (*Phyllostachys nigra*)

The black bamboo is a striking running bamboo that grows to about twenty-five feet tall. Culms are green at first but turn black over the course of their first year. Plants growing in direct sunlight show darker culms. Black bamboo is hardy to about 0° F.

Henon bamboo (*Phyllostachys nigra henonis*)

Henon bamboo is a giant running bamboo whose culms will reach four and a half inches in diameter and sixty feet high. A striking blue-gray coating contrasts with dark green leaves. Henon bamboo is hardy to −5° F.

Sasa veitchii

Sasa veitchii is a small, four-foot-tall running bamboo with attractive dark green leaves that have an interesting fall and winter effect. They develop a dry, buff-colored margin around the leaf that gives the plant a variegated appearance. It is at its most attractive in late fall and winter, when the variegation sheds light in dark places. It serves as a good woodland ground cover. *Sasa veitchii* prefers shade and is hardy to 0° F and probably root hardy to −20° F. (The photo leading this chapter is a close-up view of *Sasa veitchii*.)

Clump bamboo, or blue clump bamboo (*Fargesia nitida*, syns. *Arundinaria*, *Sinarundinaria nitida*)

Evergreen blue clump bamboo has bright green leaves and blue cast stems. It is beautiful all year long, but in late winter and early spring its delicate pale green leaves are an especially welcome sight. Not at all invasive, it forms thick clumps in sun or partial shade, growing faster in sun in a moist but well-drained soil. Very hardy (to −20° F), this clumping bamboo grows to about twenty feet. It needs a somewhat protected place, out of strong winds and also sheltered from the afternoon sun. Leaves curl in both extreme cold and hot sunlight. *Sinarundinaria nitida* is not a good plant for hot parts of the South. New canes are thin and tend to stick up, almost leafless, higher than the clump. These must *not* be cut back.

Umbrella bamboo (*Fargesia spathacea*, syn. *Thamnocalamus spathaceus*)

Umbrella bamboo is a clumping bamboo that was found by E. H. Wilson in the mountains of China. It is a delicate and graceful bamboo that is probably hardy to −20° F and grows to about fourteen feet. It requires a somewhat sheltered spot in northern gardens and prefers shade.

11. GRASSLIKE PLANTS

A FEW PLANTS look like grass and work well with grasses but belong neither to the family *Gramineae* nor to the sedge family, *Cyperaceae*. Among these are *Equisetum, Liriope, Ophiopogon,* and *Sisyrinchium*—all of which are better known by their common names: scouring rush, lily turf, mondo grass, and blue-eyed grass.

Horsetail, also called scouring rush *(Equisetum hyemale)*

Like ferns and cycads, equisetums are ancient plants that reproduce by spores rather than seeds. They belong not to *Gramineae* but to the family *Equisetaceae*. The scouring rush, an unusual-looking plant, is common to many parts of the world, and often found growing in moist places. It grows to four feet of rather hard, shiny, jointed stems of a pleasant frog-skin green. There are no leaves, so scouring rush looks a bit like bamboo canes without their foliage. It is a remarkable accent plant, with curious, very attractive jointed stems, but needs restraint because it is aggressively stoloniferous. Plant it in a sunken pot. It is hardy in Zone 4.

Lily turf *(Liriope muscari)*

As its name suggests, lily turf is a member of the lily family. Where it can be grown successfully (Zone 6), it is a tough, unde-

ABOVE: The variegated form of liriope

Sculptural horsetail, or scouring rush *(Equisetum hyemale),* noted for its aggressive growth, is contained by a handsome pot in this Los Angeles, California, garden. (Photo by Cynthia Woodyard)

Serving as a ground cover, a bank of variegated liriope brightens the space and contrasts with conifers.

Blooming when the leaves fall, green liriope is a tough, attractive evergreen ground cover or accent plant. Black berries will follow the purple flowers.

manding, extremely attractive evergreen ground cover that grows to about fourteen inches high. It blooms lavender in fall, after which rather showy black berries form. It grows in sun or shade—even dry shade, although in that position growth and size are diminished. Cut the old leaves back in spring to keep it neat-looking. There is a variegated form (shown close up in the chapter opening photo) that does better in sun.

Mondo grass (*Ophiopogon japonicus*)

Slightly less hardy than *Liriope*, mondo grass grows as far north as Zone 7. There are many cultivars of mondo grass. Two of interest are the black form, *O. planiscapus* 'Ebony Knight,' which grows to about six inches and spreads very quickly in moist, partial shade, and the very small, lustrous green *O. japonicus* 'Kyoto.' 'Kyoto' grows only about four inches tall and creeps happily between stepping stones in moist shade.

12. GRASS CARE

A s it does with any plant, caring for grasses begins with choosing the right plant for the right place. Analyze the mini-climate of your garden before choosing which grasses to grow there. Then, take into account the growth traits and limitations of your choices and what will be necessary to establish and maintain them. As a group, ornamental grasses are among the easiest of plants to grow. With a little planning and care at the outset, they will thrive in your garden for decades.

A GRASS CARE PRIMER

The following is a concise rundown of factors to take into account for success in ornamental grass culture. Attend to these basics, and Mother Nature will do the rest.

ABOVE: A cornlike frond of *Arundo donax* waves behind a clump of *Miscanthus sinensis* 'Gracillimus' (left) in the author's garden. The border planting is candytuft (*Iberis sempervirens*), with ligularia blooming in front of the miscanthus. In the background, clumps of *Miscanthus sinensis* rise above a planting of *Sedum* 'Autumn Joy.'

Selection

To get your grass garden off to the best possible start, select and procure properly labeled plants from a reputable nursery. Sometimes aggressive, running plants are sold as "pampas grass" or another vague designation. Common names are never enough to ensure the correct type of grass. If the plant you want is listed as *Miscanthus sinensis* 'Gracillimus,' ask for the plant using its entire name: its genus (*Miscanthus*), its species (*sinensis*), and the cultivar name ('Gracillimus'). "*Miscanthus*" alone refers to any number of plants, of which some are as aggressive as running bamboo. The species name, *sinensis*, narrows down the field to Eulalia grass. But it is the cultivar name, 'Gracillimus,' that designates a particular form of Eulalia—maiden grass—with exceptionally fine foliage and a graceful, vase-shaped habit.

Start with a healthy, good-sized plant, so you can quickly come to know and enjoy its natural form and beauty.

Hardiness

Check the hardiness rating of the grass you have selected. Established using data showing the lowest winter temperatures in a given area, hardiness ratings are expressed as "zones." To find your zone, look at the USDA map in the back of this book. Many ornamental grasses are hardier than they are rated in nursery catalogs. Nurseries located, for example, in Zone 6 or 7 are understandably reluctant to risk misleading customers with reports of greater hardiness than they can document themselves. Relying on the reports of people growing grasses farther north does not take into consideration the micro-climate in which a particular grass is grown. A location in the teeth of the wind, on a hill, in a frost pocket, protected by sheltering evergreens, or in a sun pocket on the south side, all create micro-climates within the larger temperature zone. Ratings are good guidelines, but they are not the last word. A gardener living in Zone 5 ought to give a grass he's wild about a try—even if it is rated "Zone 6." A winter mulch helps.

Be optimistic but reasonable in your expectations, and match the correct plant to your garden's micro-climate. A garden in dense shade will not nurture the sun-loving *Miscanthus sinensis* of your dreams. Look instead to shade-loving grasses. And vice versa.

Light

The majority of grasses prefer sun and grow bigger and more voluptuous in full sun. When grown under optimum light conditions, grasses stand tall and usually do not need support. Nevertheless, many gardeners report good luck with sun-loving grasses in situations that are considerably less than ideal. Giant miscanthus (*M. floridulus*) will grow with only two to three hours of direct sunlight or where there is bright, high shade all day long. Maiden grass (*Miscanthus sinensis* 'Gracillimus') makes a good showing under similar conditions. Of course, both would be taller, fuller, and attain greater girth faster in full sun. Where this is not the case, it is still nice to have grasses grow at all—even if more slowly and less densely.

Transplanting

Grasses need some help to get off to a good start. Water and care for seedlings and transplants as you would any newcomer to your garden. If the soil is dry when you transplant, fill a large planting hole with water before setting in the new grass. Add compost to the soil. Then fill around it with soil and water again.

Soil Fertility

Most ornamental grasses require nothing more than ordinary soil that is moderately fertile and well drained. If you coddle grasses a bit and place them in very fertile soils and give regular moisture, stand back! Growth will be markedly enhanced. In fact, giving a grass a very rich diet—or not feeding it—controls its growth.

Some grasses, the fescues and ribbon grass *(Phalaris arundinacea picta)*, tend to become rank in rich soils. Grow them in poor soil.

Drainage

Provide adequate drainage for grasses. A "moist" soil is one with a high moisture-retentive humus content, not one in standing water. Even a moisture-loving *Carex* won't stand for wet feet.

Irrigation

In dry summer climates, southern California, and climates with seasonal rainfall, non-natives need irrigation. However, grasses native to the area go dormant in the dry season and may die if they are irrigated.

In climates with year-round rainfall, established grasses do not need supplemental watering (except perhaps in the most serious droughts). What they do need is good drainage.

Form

One of the great charms of grasses is their windblown, spontaneous look. Expect them to be casual in form, and accept an occasional flop-over after a deluge.

Ornamental grasses grow into their own distinct forms without trimming of any kind. Especially when grown in part shade, some sun-lovers become floppy. Tie these to the clump or stake them if this bothers you.

Winter Care

Mulch very tender grasses and those growing north of their hardiness zone.

Grasses that are not evergreen may or may not be attractive after frost or during the dry season. Many people find some grasses, like fountain grass *(Pennisetum alopecuroides)*, Eulalia grass *(Miscanthus sinensis* and varieties), switch grass *(Panicum virgatum)*, and giant reed *(Arundo donax)* at their most beautiful in winter after their foliage has been struck by frost. Other grasses are less attractive. Whether to cut back or allow them to stand over the dormant period is a matter of taste.

Cutting Back

Be sure to cut back grasses that have been let stand over winter. Do this in late winter or the early spring *before* the new growth starts. It is much, much easier to cut straight across the old blades than around and among new ones. A combination of old and new foliage always looks messy. Use a weed trimmer to cut back a garden full of ornamental grasses.

A combination of last year's winter-blanched foliage and new growth never looks good.

New shoots of giant miscanthus (*Miscanthus floridulus*) poke out of the ground in spring. Note that the old growth has been cut back to several inches above the ground.

Some grasses don't hold together after blooming. Cut them back. Some cool-season grasses—the fescues, the mellics—look better with a little tidying up after their flower stalks turn brown and unsightly.

Brown-out

In hot climates, expect some "brown-out" from certain cool-season grasses. For example, *Arrhenatherum elatius bulbosum variegatum* simply bides its time over summer until cool weather returns again. Others, like *Holcus lanatus variegatus* or some fescues, fare worse and decline in direct proportion to rising temperatures. If the weather turns very hot and sultry, some become dormant.

In hot summer climates, with a few exceptions—notably *Calamagrostis acutiflora stricta*—think of cool-season grasses as early season ornamentals like bulbs, poppies, or peonies. Team them with more enduring partners for summer show. For example, *Festuca* and juniper combine well. After a springtime splash of showy flowers, *Festuca* may rest until cooler weather returns, but juniper will hold the fort and the form throughout the hot, hot weather.

Succession Planting

Provide early season color in the spaces left bare by warm-season grasses. Warm-season grasses don't even show signs of growth until

Warm-season grasses start growth in the late spring. Emerging fountain grass (*Pennisetum alopecuroides*) grows between blooming tulips and the foliage of soon-to-bloom Persian alliums. By the time the alliums bloom, the fountain grass will have covered the ground.

the weather settles. The truly delightful alternative to the bare spot left by a shorn and dormant grass is a succession of bulbs. This combination works so well that it is hard to think of grass without bulbs. Start with very early bulbs like the glory-of-the-snow (*Chionodoxa*), which spreads nicely and covers the ground around the dormant grass like a blue carpet. Bulbs are perfect for this role, but perennials that die back after flowering (Oriental poppies, Virginia bluebells, etc.) are other possibilities.

Camouflage

Early blooming plants do in the grasses' absence what grasses do for the bulbs' after-bloom dishevelment. When bulbs and spring blooming plants are not at their best, when they become messy or brown out or go dormant, warm-season grasses grow up into fresh, clean, attractive cover around them.

Spacing

When warm-season grasses finally do begin their growth, they shoot up quickly. Their total growth over the space of a single season is amazingly profuse. It is often difficult in the bareness of early spring to comprehend how much room they actually will require, but it is important to allot them space.

Give grasses enough room to grow. Like many perennials, they will not approach their full growth until their third year in the ground. It is always hard to imagine how big they will ultimately be. Kurt Bluemel's rule of spacing plants as far apart as they will become tall is a safe one to follow.

Division and Transplanting

Divide or transplant cool-season grasses in fall, late winter, or early spring. Divide and transplant warm-season grasses in early spring.

Large grasses like *Miscanthus sinensis* and *Erianthus* change character over the years. A clump of *M. sinensis* 'Gracillimus' in its second or third year in the garden will have a very upright, narrow vase shape. After ten years in one place, it will have grown into a ring—empty in the center—that is perhaps six feet in diameter. This older grass has a powerful and very attractive character, but if what you want is the lissome, slender young grass, dig up the clump and cut it into small sections.

Grasses from Seed

Many grasses grow easily from seed. Foremost among these is perennial fountain grass (*Pennisetum alopecuroides*) and the different types of annual fountain grasses, *Pennisetum setaceum* and *Pennisetum villosum*. Started in late winter, perennial *P. alopecuroides* will reach eighteen inches or more in its first season and produce a few flowers. It goes almost without saying that any grass that starts this easily also self-sows. However, the young seedlings are not difficult to uproot. Grasses that grow from seed include *Stipa gigantea*, *Panicum virgatum*, *Miscanthus sinensis*, *Briza media*, *Carex muskingumensis*, *Carex pendula*, *Chasmanthium latifolium*, *Cortaderia selloana*, and *Koeleria*.

Some self-sowers need to be controlled. Plan a mid- to late spring weeding around prolific self-sowers like *Pennisetum alopecuroides* and *Chasmanthium latifolium*. Using a mulch around self-sowers is also helpful.

Cultivars like *Miscanthus sinensis* 'Gracillimus,' or *Miscanthus sinensis* 'Morning Light' have to be vegetatively propagated. It is not possible to grow them from seed. But it is fascinating to raise a batch of *Miscanthus sinensis* seedlings and observe the differences in habit and size. Of ten, one or two may have very narrow foliage—not unlike *M. sinensis* 'Gracillimus'; another may show a stockier, broad-leafed form; and the rest might look very like the straight species.

Divide cultivars (e.g., *M. sinensis* 'Gracillimus,' *M. sinensis* 'Silberfeder') to increase the number of plants.

ADVICE FROM THE EXPERTS

Kurt Bluemel—General Care Guidelines

Kurt Bluemel, whose nursery offers the largest selection of ornamental grasses in the United States, suggests the following guidelines for growing ornamental grasses: "Use the same kind of cultural practice as you would use in growing, cultivating, and maintaining perennials. I cannot emphasize it enough: They belong exactly in that group of plants."

As noted earlier, Mr. Bluemel suggests that grasses should be positioned as far apart as they are tall—"if a plant is six feet, plant it six feet apart. This is a good rule of thumb." However, he is quick to point out that the distance allowed between plants really "depends on what you want to do. If you want to have a plant covering large areas, you space more closely." (See Kurt Bluemel's design suggestions in chapter 4, "Designing with Ornamental Grasses.")

He recommends dividing grasses infrequently. "I would think that a miscanthus or a pennisetum could stand in the same place for a decade. There's no call for dividing if you have planned correctly" and given them enough room to grow—"a massive plant like that needs space." Again, he points out, it depends upon the design. "If you want to keep a small-sized clump, then you have to replant every so often and 'every so often' is definitely not every two years."

"Another important point," he adds, "is when to plant, transplant, or divide the grasses." This depends upon "what groups they are in," whether cool- or warm-season. "If you plant pennisetum in November, you're going to lose it. It's the same with *Arundo donax* and all of those tropical-looking, warm-season grasses that totally disappear in the ground. They need spring planting."

On the other hand, he advises, "don't divide your *Festuca* in the middle of the summer. It's a cool-season grass. Wait until fall. Cool-season grasses are sort of evergeen." To determine whether a grass is a cool- or warm-season grower, he suggests investigation. "It's a logical kind of thing—if something shows growth in fall, you know damn well it will grow in cool weather. That's a very simple thing to see."

Grasses that don't receive enough light do not stand tall, but flop over. When you see this, he says, "it's time to move the tree! When ornamental grasses are grown in concert with trees and shrubs," he says, "the trees and shrubs grow almost as much as the grasses and slowly shade them out. So what you do is either redecorate—replant—or you reduce the overhead shade or just use a different kind of grass that grows well in shade. That's part of the redecorating."

One group of grasses that requires particular care is the blue grasses. "Blue grasses . . . coat themselves with a bluish gray waxy coat," he says. "They protect themselves from evaporation, so they are somewhat moisture-sensitive. You want to ensure good drainage for them."

Finally, Mr. Bluemel notes that while a grass like *Erianthus ravennae* can be kept to a manageable size by "keeping it a little hungry," most grasses benefit from a slow-release fertilizer. Another method of containing big grasses, he adds, is by literally containing them in bottomless halves of five-gallon drums.

Richard A. Simon—Basic Pointers

Richard A. Simon is owner of Bluemount Nurseries, Inc. (wholesale only) in Monkton, Maryland. Bluemount was the first nursery in the United States in recent years to assemble a collection of ornamental grasses. Mr. Simon began growing grasses in the early 1960s, gathering some from around the country and importing others from Europe. He says, "I was attracted by their beauty, their ever-changing nature, and their winter interest."

Today, Bluemount Nurseries lists among its offerings of perennials, vines, bamboo, and ground cover plants a choice selection of ornamental grasses. Mr. Simon concentrates on grasses he knows will survive without question for his customers.

"For me," he says, "*Cortaderia selloana* [pampas grass] is a big question mark." He notes that a return to very cold winters might well kill plants now growing in the Baltimore–Washington, D.C., area.

He suggests that gardeners choose a clumping rather than a running grass. He also advises planting grasses "with a lot of organic matter. The grass, which will stay in the same place for a decade or more, responds to organic matter."

Keeping ornamental grasses mulched is another recommendation. "They will tolerate a lot of mulch," he says, but he cautions against using too much nitrogen. "It is going to make them weak, and storms will blow them over." Instead, he advises a slow-release fertilizer—"either an organic or resin-coated one that is low in nitrogen in early spring."

"Grasses are drought resistant," he observes, and sees "no problem in transplanting when dormant."

Aside from that, he feels that "the only thing you have to do is keep them mulched, plant sun-loving varieties in the sun, cut them back in early spring, and divide them ten years down the road." Division is a project that involves "digging up and dividing a big clump into smaller sections with an axe."

Cool green and white *Phalaris arundinacea picta,* growing in a Long Island flower border, becomes coarse and rank if grown in a rich soil. To improve the appearance of tired-looking *Phalaris,* some gardeners mow it down or cut it back completely to grow a crop of fresh, new foliage.

Pauline Vollmer—Maintenance Needs

Pauline Vollmer of Baltimore has enjoyed ornamental grasses in her garden for twenty-six years. It was in 1962 that Wolfgang Oehme, as yet not in business for himself, "did a little design for the terrace by the house," remembers Mrs. Vollmer. "It was such an unusual design" that she recalls being taken aback at first and then deciding with her husband that "we both liked it so much we went ahead and did the whole garden." Since that time, she has enjoyed her garden immensely.

"Before I give advice on caring for grasses," she says, "I would like to say why I like growing grasses: Grasses add grace to a garden that you don't get in many other plants. They bring pleasant motion and move and sway in the slightest breeze. Some of them give a little sound.

"Grasses give a rather constant landscape. They're there most of the year. Most are at their peak in later summer, when other plants look shabby, and they offer quite a bit of winter interest."

One of the reasons that Pauline Vollmer enjoys her garden so much is that it requires relatively little maintenance. "If we want to have nice gardens, we have to be sensible and grow things we can take care of ourselves," she says, adding, "It's common sense. People do not have gardeners anymore."

"Grasses resist diseases and insects," she continues. "It's really true! Most everything has bug bites at this time of year, but you don't see bug bites on grasses. They also tolerate drought well and don't need transplanting or division. They require very little pruning except cutting down annually. The medium ones are wonderful for hiding dying bulbs' foliage [and] the smaller ones like *Carex morrowii variegata* hide fallen tree leaves. *Carex morrowii variegata*," says Mrs. Vollmer, "is wonderful. It just sits there. I haven't done a thing to it."

Having carefree grasses and perennials in the garden "enables me to have a garden that gives me pleasure all year around without having to use chemicals of which I'm not in favor. There is no feeding, spraying, and weed killing in any way."

In twenty-six years, Pauline Vollmer has never fertilized her ornamental grasses. "If I fertilized," she says, "they'd be even bigger and more trouble tying up."

In terms of maintenance—besides cutting the grasses back each year, which she says is "a must"—her only real problem is propping up floppy twenty-six-year-old grasses. Over the years she and her late husband developed several methods for keeping the grasses standing at attention. For a mighty stand of giant miscanthus, her husband sank pipes into the ground permanently so that they were slightly protruding above the surface. Whenever the giant miscanthus needed restraining, he used the sunken pipes to hold temporary supports made from pipes of slightly smaller diameter. To these he strung plastic-coated wire.

For smaller grasses like spodiopogon and *Miscanthus purpurascens*, Mrs. Vollmer fashions a girdle of wire fencing. "If you do it early enough," she says, "the leaves go through it and hide it."

This year she also took two-inch square wire fencing, bent it, and placed it over the top of a grass, anchoring the wire with stakes. "It will hold the grass nicely and will look very natural for a long time."

Another method of keeping growth reasonably in bounds is by breaking (not cutting) off the outside stems. "I break them off or bend them down and walk off and leave them and later cut them back." Wounding the grass in this way discourages growth, while clean cutting does not.

Mrs. Vollmer acknowledges that grasses—especially very old grasses—have a tendency to spread out or flop over. But their other attributes far outweigh the negative. "If I hadn't thought they were worth it, I wouldn't have grown them for twenty-five years."

John Greenlee—Grasses for Dry Climates

John Greenlee, horticulturist, designer, and nurseryman, grows and sells grasses at his nursury, John Greenlee & Associates in Pomona, California. It is located "over two ridges from the Pacific coast." He describes the climate: "In summer the average temperature is around 90 degrees [Fahrenheit], but there's a big range. It fluctuates, reaching as low as 28 to 29 degrees—and it has gone down to 18 degrees. Many grasses do just as well here [as farther north]. Most have good fall color."

The main difference between southern California and most of the country is that rains are seasonal in the Southwest. There is no rain at all from about June until November.

"Los Angeles," says Mr. Greenlee, "is a desert." He would like people—particularly Easterners—to know that "the whole country doesn't have green as a summer color. A garden in the traditional sense . . . doesn't exist without water." The desire to have a traditional garden despite the desert climate, he explains, is why so many people irrigate lawns every day in southern California.

"We are looking for drought-tolerant lawn substitutes that only need water once every two weeks or once each week and a half. Once each week would be a tremendous savings," he says. One promising lawn substitute is mosquito grass *(Bouteloua gracilis)*, a native. "Green without a lot of water is going to be a big ticket here in the West."

Ornamental grasses have to be irrigated in southern California, but some are more tolerant of drought than others. Others, like the genus *Carex*, need plentiful water. Most of them also need shade. *Molinia* Mr. Greenlee describes as being "slow to establish" but fine once it is established. *Milium effusum aureum* "really needs moisture and shade. *Hakonechloa macra* (the green form) is a superb grass for the West (unlike the variegated form). *Festuca amesthystina* 'Bronzeglanz' is the best flowering fescue for us."

Some grasses grow *too well* in southern California. "Bermuda grass is the worst pest that we have in southern California. It is rampant. Lawn services can bring in pieces on lawnmowers and infect new areas." Before anyone can even think about growing ornamental grasses, he has to get rid of Bermuda grass. "This will take a series of herbicide and irrigation and herbicide and irrigation

Tough, drought-tolerant lyme grass *(Elymus glaucus)*, a North American dune grass, teams with agaves in an easy-care beach house planting in Malibu, California. (Design and photo: John Greenlee)

until it is controlled. Once Bermuda grass gets in there," he says, "you'll never get rid of it."

Another pest grass is pampas grass *(Cortaderia).* John Greenlee says that he isn't sure whether the pampas grass that has escaped is the species *selloana,* but adds that he would not trust "anybody's clone of it." He is observing *Cortaderia pumila,* a species that doesn't have "the seeding habit—at least it doesn't come up from seed for us"—as a replacement.

He remembers as a child learning of *Arundo donax* as "one of the pests of agriculture. It was brought by the Spanish mission fathers, who used it to build animal pens, for windbreaks, and for baskets and weaving.

"Any plant out of place can be a pest," he says. "If something does seed itself, be careful." In using self-sowers, he advises proceeding "with great caution. We have to pay attention to how we use it. I have had to approach this situation on a case by case basis.

"As a horticulturist," says Mr. Greenlee, "I think it's important to know a little bit more about plants before we throw them out on the general public. My great fear is having some grass I've brought in be given my name as a common name—like 'Greenlee's Scourge.'"

What is a weed in southern California may be difficult to grow in another region. Grasses change in growth patterns, sizes, or even color—sometimes dramatically—from region to region. "There are definite regional differences," says Mr. Greenlee, "no matter where you are. In southern California, deschampsias grow but are not strong bloomers." Recalling a trip to Portland, Oregon, where he observed deschampsia growing in a field, he says, "They really lived up to their names." A plant like 'Goldschleier' really did suggest a golden veil. They did what they were supposed to do. "Late-blooming ones came out late. They definitely look better in Portland, Oregon, than in southern California.

"We are a bit worried about *Imperata,*" he says. "We've had a reversion. If it reverts in a mild climate, that will be a problem. The native *Imperata* is very aggressive.

"We're noticing with some regularity that clumps of *Miscanthus sinensis* including the cultivar 'Gracillimus' after the third year do not want to stand up. But," he points out, "plants that spill over are great for hills." He notes two grasses that don't do well. "*Carex buchananii* lasts for two or three years and then the clump dies. Variegated hakonechloa doesn't like the hot climate."

Another example of different behavior in a different region is provided by *Miscanthus sinensis purpurascens.* "It just does not do anything here in southern California at the low elevation," he says. "It might do very well in the foothills of the Sierras or any place in California where it is colder. By the time you get to Portland, it's fabulous—a glorious, compact little miscanthus with that rich foliage color and that great fall color. It colors for us," he says, "but is just a weaker plant and it does not want to go dry in any way, shape, or form. *Purpurascens* won't take it here."

The plants that will take it—the months of heat without water—are the natives, most of which go dormant over the summer. "We are pursuing the native grasses here," says Mr. Greenlee.

Unlike ornamental grasses that originate in regions with more regular rainfall around the year, dry climate natives can succumb to rot if they are watered in summer. For this reason they cannot be grouped with plants that are drought resistant but need occasional watering. John Greenlee is interested in native grasses "from the fringes" of a dry summer area that can take both "dry or additional summer water." *Muhlenbergia* and some native *Calamagrostis* are very promising. "It's just a matter of time before someone starts growing them."

CHOOSING GRASSES FOR DRY CLIMATES

These are John Greenlee's evaluations of grasses suited to dry climates like that of southern California:

The Most Drought-Tolerant Grasses

☐ *Andropogon*—"We're excited about it; it's quite drought tolerant."
☐ *Bouteloua gracilis*
☐ *Chasmanthium latifolium*—"It may not look good, but it will still get by."
☐ *Panicum virgatum*—"In a really dry situation they are miniaturized but look fine."

Somewhat Drought-Tolerant Grasses

☐ *Miscanthus sinensis*—"It can handle the dry, but prefers moisture. The cultivars 'Silver Feather' and 'Morning Light' are excellent."
☐ *Spartina pectinata aureo-marginata*—"It grows in a dry situation or in water. It does well no matter where you put it."
☐ *Stipa gigantea*—"Stipas are tricky; they need good drainage and not much water."
☐ *Pennisetum alopecuroides*—"It takes the dry, but shows it. It prefers water."

Grasses That Self-Sow and Escape in Southern California

In a dry, sunny climate, use these grasses with great care or choose nonseeding alternatives.

□ *Arundo donax*
□ Bermuda grass
□ *Cortaderia*—"but not 'Pumila' —not yet anyway."
□ *Pennisetum setaceum*—"It has naturalized in southern California."
□ *Pennisetum incomptum*
□ *Pennisetum alopecuroides* 'Moudry'—"but not *P. alopecuroides* or *P. a.* 'Hameln.'"
□ *Pennisetum villosum*—"It has naturalized in southern California."
□ *Erianthus ravennae*
□ *Panicum virgatum*—"but not 'Haense Herms.'"

Mary Hockenberry Meyer—Grasses for Cold Climates

Mary Hockenberry Meyer is a horticulturist who was an early ornamental grass enthusiast. She has written and lectured extensively on ornamental grasses and is currently pursuing a doctorate at the University of Minnesota, where she is evaluating the cold hardiness of grasses and studying the flowering and genetics of ornamental pennisetum. She also tends several hundred grasses in Minnesota, "a rigorous climate," where −25° Fahrenheit is "a normal winter minimum," but where intense heat in summer is common: "This year [1988] we have had forty-two days of 90 degrees Fahrenheit or more. The normal number of 90-plus degrees Fahrenheit days is probably about twenty."

The hot summers of the Plains states encourage "the growth of warm-season grasses: miscanthus, pennisetum, *Erianthus*," she observes, describing that growth as "very rapid, similar to [that in] a Zone 6 climate in the summer.

"Fescues, *Helictotrichon sempervirens*, *Elymus glaucus*, *Koeleria*, *Phalaris*, and *Deschampsia* are all cool-season grasses that have good cold hardiness; they flower early and often go dormant or semidormant in the heat of the summer.

"The native prairie warm-season grasses—*Panicum*, *Spartina*, *Andropogon*, *Schizachryium*, *Bouteloua*, and *Sorghastrum*—are true champions of adverse conditions. Despite severe winters, they come back year after year, and with hot summers they flourish.

"*Miscanthus sinensis purpurascens* appears to be one of the hardiest miscanthus and, being an early flowering type, it is especially attractive for Minnesota."

Some plants will not grow in her Minnesota garden. Pampas grass (*Cortaderia selloana*) is one of them. The dwarf forms of miscanthus—*Miscanthus oligostachys* and 'Yaku Jima'—are others. The variegated form of *Arundo donax* was yet another casualty to cold. She adds, "The green form of *Arundo* survived here last year, but I would not bet on it again." Amazingly, blood grass (*Imperata cylindrica)*, a native of central Africa, made it. "Cold protection," she states, "is important here."

She offers the following tips for growing grasses in a cold climate. "Questionably hardy types like the variegated miscanthus *(Miscanthus sinensis variegatus)* need protection—northern exposure with snow cover and/or winter mulch. A snow cover is a big help. Winds are very strong here in the winter. Therefore if snowfall isn't heavy, plants are often exposed. Corners or northern exposures where snow collects will help increase plants' survival rate.

"Fall planting in Zone 4 is a risk. Spring is safer. Plant bare root grasses [mail order plants] as soon as possible, and soak roots overnight prior to planting. Bare root plants—grasses, perennials, whatever—need all the help they can get at planting time.

"*Pennisetum alopecuroides* is not one hundred percent hardy here. Often it needs protection. I hope to select hardy forms of this type and look at crossing it with *P. setaceum* for a longer period of bloom."

CHOOSING GRASSES FOR COLD CLIMATES

Mary Hockenberry Meyer has drawn up the following lists of grasses recommended for cold climates based on what she calls "limited knowledge." She says, "I like to be conservative in my recommendations," but suspects that the plants marked with an asterisk on the Zone 4 list can also be grown in Zone 3, especially in protected sites.

Best Grasses for Zone 4 (− 20° to − 30° F)

- ☐ *Arrhenatherum elatius bulbosum variegatum*
- ☐ *Alopecurus pratensis aureus*
- ☐ *Calamagrostis acutiflora stricta*
- ☐ *Calamagrostis arundinacea brachytricha*
- ☐ *Carex flava*
- ☐ *Carex morrowii* 'Old Gold' (with protection)
- ☐ *Carex muskingumensis*
- ☐ *Carex nigra*
- ☐ *Chasmanthium latifolium*
- ☐ *Deschampsia caespitosa*
- ☐ *Eragrostis trichodes*
- ☐ *Erianthus ravennae* (with protection)
- ☐ *Hakonechloa macra* (with protection)
- ☐ *Hakonechloa macra aureola* (with protection)
- ☐ *Hystrix patula*
- ☐ *Imperata cylindrica* (with protection)

☐ *Miscanthus sinensis* (most cultivars; variegated miscanthus needs protection)
☐ **Molinea caerulea* and variants
☐ *Pennisetum alopecuroides* (may need protection)
☐ *Sesleria* species
☐ *Spodiopogon sibericus*

Best Grasses for Zone 3 (− 30° to − 40° F)

☐ *Andropogon gerardi*
☐ *Bouteloua curtipendula*
☐ *Bouteloua gracilis*
☐ *Deschampsia caespitosa*
☐ *Elymus giganteus*
☐ *Elymus glaucus*
☐ *Festuca* (probably all species)
☐ *Helictotrichon sempervirens*
☐ *Koeleria glauca*
☐ *Miscanthus sacchariflorus*
☐ *Panicum virgatum*
☐ *Phalaris arundinacea picta*
☐ *Schizachyrium scoparium* (*Andropogon scoparius*)
☐ *Sorghastrum nutans*
☐ *Spartina pectinata aureomarginata*

OPPOSITE: *Miscanthus sinensis condensatus* as a spot screen next to a parking area in the author's garden. At left, a planting of *Pennisetum villosum* started from seed several months before the picture was taken.

APPENDIXES

A. GRASSES FOR USE IN THE LANDSCAPE

L IMEROCK ORNAMENTAL GRASSES, INC., of Port Matilda, Pennsylvania, offers a highly refined selection of ornamental grasses. Owner Norman Hooven states he does not try to "offer every grass currently available." His selection is listed in the Limerock catalog, itself an excellent primer on the culture of ornamental grasses and outstanding in its articulate descriptions. Reprinted with kind permission from the Limerock catalog are Mr. Hooven's suggestions for the landscape use of grasses and lists of grasses with particular soil requirements. (Lists include only those grasses included in this book and, in some cases, botanical spelling has been changed for consistency.)

SPECIMENS

Arundo donax
Erianthus ravennae
Imperata cylindrica 'Red Baron'
Miscanthus species
Pennisetum alopecuroides
Pennisetum orientale

BORDERS

Arrhenatherum elatius bulbosum variegatum
Calamagrostis acutiflora stricta
Carex buchananii
Carex morrowii variegata and *C. morrowii aureo-variegata*
Deschampsia caespitosa
Festuca species
Helictotrichon sempervirens
Imperata cylindrica 'Red Baron'
Koeleria glauca
Miscanthus species
Panicum virgatum
Sisyrinchium angustifolium

ROCK GARDENS

Arrhenatherum elatius bulbosum variegatum
Bouteloua gracilis
Briza media
Carex buchananii
Festuca species
Helictotrichon sempervirens
Holcus lanatus variegatus
Imperata cylindrica 'Red Baron'
Koeleria glauca
Melica ciliata
Sisyrinchium angustifolium

GROUND COVERS

Arrhenatherum elatius bulbosum variegatum
Carex morrowii variegata and *C. morrowii aureo-variegata*
Carex nigra
Festuca species
Holcus lanatus variegatus
Koeleria glauca

EDGING

Carex morrowii variegata and *C. morrowii aureo-variegata*
Festuca species
Holcus lanatus variegatus
Koeleria glauca

SCREENS AND HEDGES

Arundo donax
Calamagrostis acutiflora stricta
Chasmanthium latifolium
Deschampsia caespitosa
Erianthus ravennae
Miscanthus species
Panicum virgatum and cultivars
Spartina pectinata aureo-marginata

BACKGROUND PLANTINGS

Arundo donax
Calamagrostis acutiflora stricta
Erianthus ravennae
Miscanthus species
Molinia caerulea arundinacea 'Windspiel'
Panicum virgatum
Spartina pectinata aureo-marginata

WOODLAND SETTINGS

Carex morrowii variegata and *C. morrowii aureo-variegata*
Carex nigra
Chasmanthium latifolium
Sisyrinchium angustifolium

BEACH HOUSE PLANTINGS

Bouteloua gracilis
Chasmanthium latifolium
Elymus glaucus
Holcus lanatus
Miscanthus species
Phalaris arundinacea picta
Spartina pectinata aureo-marginata

GROUPS, MASSING

Arrhenatherum elatius bulbosum variegatum
Bouteloua gracilis
Briza media
Carex buchananii
Carex morrowii variegata
Carex nigra
Chasmanthium latifolium
Elymus glaucus
Festuca species
Helictotrichon sempervirens
Melica ciliata
Miscanthus species
Molinia caerulea arundinacea 'Windspiel'
Panicum virgatum
Phalaris arundinacea picta

WATERSIDE PLANTINGS

Arundo donax
Calamagrostis acutiflora stricta
Chasmanthium latifolium
Deschampsia caespitosa
Erianthus ravennae
Melica ciliata
Miscanthus species (*M. sinensis* 'Gracillimus' best for drying)

GRASSES WITH PARTICULAR SOIL REQUIREMENTS

☐ These grasses should be grown in poor soil—growth becomes coarse in good soils:

Briza media
Bouteloua gracilis—light, sandy, acidic soil
Festuca species—light, loamy soil
Phalaris arundinacea picta

☐ These grasses should be grown in light, sandy soil:

Holcus lanatus variegatus
Spartina pectinata aureo-marginata

☐ These grasses will tolerate very heavy clay soils:

Calamagrostis acutiflora stricta
Deschampsia caespitosa
Elymus glaucus
Phalaris arundinacea picta

☐ These grasses should be grown in soil high in lime:

Koeleria glauca
Melica ciliata

☐ These grasses do best in deeply cultivated soil that is high in organic matter:

Erianthus ravennae
Miscanthus sinensis (all varieties)

B. GRASS CHART

BOTANICAL NAME	SIZE				FOLIAGE COLOR				TYPE			EXPOSURE		
	Small: Under 12"	Medium: 1–3'	Large: 3–6'	Giant: 6'+	Blue/gray	Variegated	Yellow/Yellow-green	Red/Brown	Warm-season	Cool-season	Evergreen/Semi-evergreen	Sun	Shade	Half-shade
Alopecurus pratensis aureus		*					*			*		*		*
Andropogon scoparius (Schizacheium scoparium)		*							*			*		
Arundo donax				*	*				*			*		
Arundo donax variegata				*		*			*			*		
Arrhenatherum elatius bulbosum variegatum	*					*				*		*		*
Bouteloua gracilis		*							*			*		
Briza media		*								*		*		
Calamagrostis acutiflora stricta			*							*		*		
Calamagrostis arundinacea brachytricha		*							*			*		*
Carex buchananii		*						*	*	*	*	*		
Carex conica-marginata	*					*					*		*	*
Carex morrowii variegata		*				*					*		*	*
Carex morrowii aureo-variegata		*				*					*		*	*
Carex muskingumensis		*								*			*	*
Carex nigra	*				*						*		*	*
Carex ornithopoda variegata	*					*					*		*	*
Carex pendula		*									*		*	*
Carex stricta 'Bowles Golden' (Carex elata)	*						*			*			*	*
Chasmanthium latifolium (Uniola)		*							*			*	*	*
Cortaderia selloana				*	*				*			*		
Deschampsia caespitosa		*									*		*	*
Elymus glaucus		*			*				*			*		
Erianthus ravennae				*	*				*			*		
Festuca amethystina 'Superba'	*				*					*		*		

BLOOM			USE					CHARACTERISTICS							EFFECTIVE				Comments
Spring	Summer	Fall	Meadow	Specimen/Accent	Screen/Hedge	Ground Cover	Rock Garden	Hardy in Zone	Bouquets	Runner	Clumper	May brown out in hot summers	Self-sows	Native	Spring	Summer	Fall	Winter	
*			*			*		6	*		*				*	*	*		
	*		*	*		*		4–3			*			*		*	*	*	
		*		*	*			6–5	*		*					*	*	*	
		*		*	*			7–6	*		*					*	*	*	
*			*	*		*	*	4		*		*			*	*	*		
	*		*	*		*	*	4–3			*			*		*	*		Drought tolerant
	*		*			*	*	4	*		*		*			*	*		
	*		*	*	*	*	*	4	*		*				*	*	*	*	Outstanding all-around grass
		*		*			*	5	*		*					*	*	*	
	*		*	*		*	*	6			*				*	*	*	*	Brown grass
*						*	*	5			*				*	*	*	*	
*				*		*	*	5			*				*	*	*	*	
*				*		*	*	5			*				*	*	*	*	
*						*		5	*				*			*	*		Feathery foilage
*				*		*	*	6	*				*		*	*	*	*	
*				*		*	*	7			*				*	*	*	*	
*				*			*	5			*		*		*	*	*		Dramatic in bloom
*			*	*		*	*	7			*	*			*	*	*		Pure golden yellow
	*		*	*		*	*	4–3	*		*		*	*		*	*	*	Protect from wind
		*		*	*			8	*		*		*			*	*	*	
*			*			*	*	4–3			*	*	*	*	*	*	*	*	Likes moisture
	*		*	*		*	*	1–3		*				*		*	*		Very aggressive
		*		*	*			4	*		*					*	*	*	
*			*	*		*	*	4			*	*			*	*	*		

Botanical name	SIZE				FOLIAGE COLOR				TYPE			EXPOSURE		
	Small: Under 12"	Medium: 1–3'	Large: 3–6'	Giant: 6'+	Blue/gray	Variegated	Yellow/Yellow-green	Red/Brown	Warm-season	Cool-season	Evergreen/Semi-evergreen	Sun	Shade	Half-shade
Festuca cinerea 'April Gruen'	*				*					*		*		
Festuca muelleri	*									*		*		
Festuca ovina 'Solling'	*				*					*		*		
Festuca scoparia 'Pic Carlit'	*									*		*	*	*
Hakonechloa macra		*								*				*
Hakonechloa macra aureola		*				*				*				*
Helictotrichon sempervirens		*			*					*	*			
Holcus lanatus variegatus	*					*				*		*		*
Hystrix patula	*									*			*	*
Imperata cylindrica 'Red Baron'		*						*	*			*		*
Koeleria argentea		*			*					*		*		
Koeleria glauca	*				*					*		*		
Luzula pilosa	*										*		*	*
Luzula sylvatica		*									*		*	*
Melica ciliata		*								*		*		*
Melica transylvanica		*								*		*		*
Milium effusum aureum		*					*			*				*
Miscanthus floridulus				*					*			*		*
Miscanthus sacchariflorus			*						*			*		
Miscanthus sinensis				*					*			*		
Miscanthus sinensis condensatus				*					*			*		
Miscanthus sinensis 'Gracillimus'				*					*			*		
Miscanthus sinensis 'Morning Light'			*			*			*			*		
Miscanthus sinensis purpurascens			*						*			*		

Spring	Summer	Fall	Meadow	Specimen/Accent	Screen/Hedge	Ground Cover	Rock Garden	Hardy in Zone	Bouquets	Runner	Clumper	May brown out in hot summers	Self-sows	Native	Spring	Summer	Fall	Winter	Comments
*			*	*		*	*	4			*	*			*	*	*		
*						*	*	5			*					*	*		Drought tolerant
			*	*		*	*	5			*				*	*	*		Seldom blooms
	*					*	*	4							*	*	*		Brilliant green
	*			*		*	*	4			*					*	*	*	
	*			*		*	*	4			*	*				*	*	*	
*			*	*		*	*	4	*		*				*	*	*	*	
	*			*		*	*	4		*		*			*	*	*		
	*		*	*		*	*	4	*		*	*		*	*	*	*		
	*		*	*		*	*	5–4		*						*	*		Bright red
*			*	*		*	*	6–5			*	*			*	*	*		Grows in poor soil
*			*	*		*	*	4–3			*		*		*	*	*		
*						*	*	3		*			*		*	*	*	*	
*						*	*	5	*	*			*		*	*	*	*	
*			*	*		*	*	5	*		*	*			*	*	*		Good small specimen
*			*	*		*	*	5	*		*				*	*	*		
*			*	*		*	*	5		*		*			*	*	*		Bright yellow-green
		*		*	*			6	*		*					*	*	*	Good screen
		*				*		4	*	*						*	*	*	Very aggressive
		*		*	*			4	*		*		*			*	*	*	
	*			*	*			4	*	*						*	*	*	Blooms early
		*		*	*			5–4	*		*		*			*	*	*	
		*		*				5	*		*					*	*	*	Delicate appearance
	*		*	*		*		4	*		*					*	*	*	Red-orange fall color

Botanical name	SIZE				FOLIAGE COLOR				TYPE			EXPOSURE		
	Small: Under 12"	Medium: 1–3'	Large: 3–6'	Giant: 6'+	Blue/gray	Variegated	Yellow/Yellow-green	Red/Brown	Warm-season	Cool-season	Evergreen/Semi-evergreen	Sun	Shade	Half-shade
Miscanthus sinensis 'Silberfeder'				*					*			*		
Miscanthus sinensis variegatus			*			*			*			*		*
Miscanthus sinensis strictus			*			*	*		*			*		
Molinia caerulea arundinacea 'Windspiel'				*					*			*		*
Panicum virgatum			*						*			*		*
Panicum virgatum 'Haense Herms'			*						*			*		
Panicum virgatum 'Strictum'			*		*				*			*		*
Pennisetum alopecuroides		*							*			*		
P. alopecuroides 'Hameln'		*							*			*		
P. alopecuroides viridescens		*							*			*		
Pennisetum caudatum		*							*			*		
Pennisetum incomptum (flaccidum)			*						*			*		
Pennisetum orientale		*							*			*		
Pennisetum setaceum 'Cupreum' and 'Rubrum'		*						*	*			*		
Phalaris arundinacea picta		*				*				*	*	*	*	*
Phragmites australis				*					*			*		
Sesleria autumnalis		*					*		*			*		*
Sorghastrum nutans (Chrysopogon nutans)			*						*			*		
Spartina pectinata aureo-marginata			*			*			*			*		*
Spodiopogon sibiricus (Achnatherum, Muehlenbergia)			*							*		*	*	*
Sporobolus heterolepsis		*							*			*		
Stipa gigantea			*		*					*		*		

BLOOM			USE					CHARACTERISTICS							EFFECTIVE				Comments
Spring	Summer	Fall	Meadow	Specimen/Accent	Screen/Hedge	Ground Cover	Rock Garden	Hardy in Zone	Bouquets	Runner	Clumper	May brown out in hot summers	Self-sows	Native	Spring	Summer	Fall	Winter	
	*			*	*			5–4	*		*					*	*	*	Blooms early
		*		*	*			6	*		*					*	*	*	
		*		*	*			6	*		*					*	*	*	
*			*	*				4	*		*					*	*		Kinetic sculpture
*	*		*	*		*		3		*			*	*		*	*	*	Outstanding winter appearance
*			*	*		*		3		*			*	*		*	*	*	Red autumn color
*			*	*		*		3		*				*		*	*	*	Very hardy
*			*	*		*	*	5–4	*		*		*			*	*	*	Outstanding landscape grass
*			*	*		*	*	5	*		*		*			*	*	*	
*			*	*		*	*	7	*		*		*			*	*	*	
*			*	*		*	*	5	*		*					*	*	*	
*			*			*		6–5		*						*	*	*	Aggressive
*			*	*		*	*	7	*		*					*	*	*	Early bloomer
*			*	*		*	*	8	*		*					*	*		Annuals
*			*			*	*	4–3		*					*	*	*		Aggressive
*			*	*	*	*		4–3		*			*	*		*	*	*	Tolerates wet situations
		*	*	*		*	*	5			*					*	*		
*			*	*		*	*	3	*		*	*	*	*		*	*	*	Extremely hardy, drought tolerant
		*	*		*		*	3	*	*			*	*		*	*	*	Yellow fall color
		*		*	*			4	*		*					*	*		
*			*	*		*		4	*		*		*	*		*	*	*	Outstanding native appearance
*			*	*		*	*	7	*		*	*			*	*	*		Spectacular blooms, needs good drainage

C. HARDINESS ZONE MAP

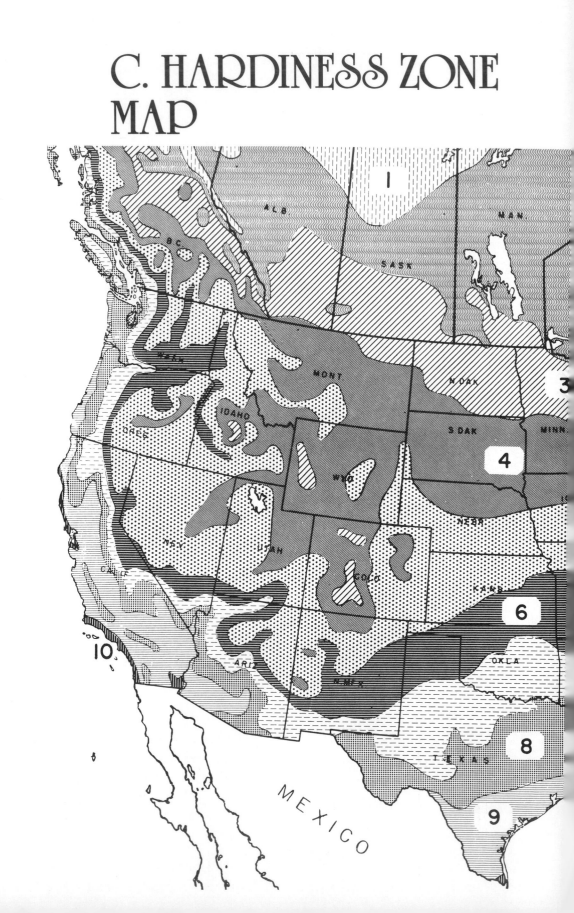

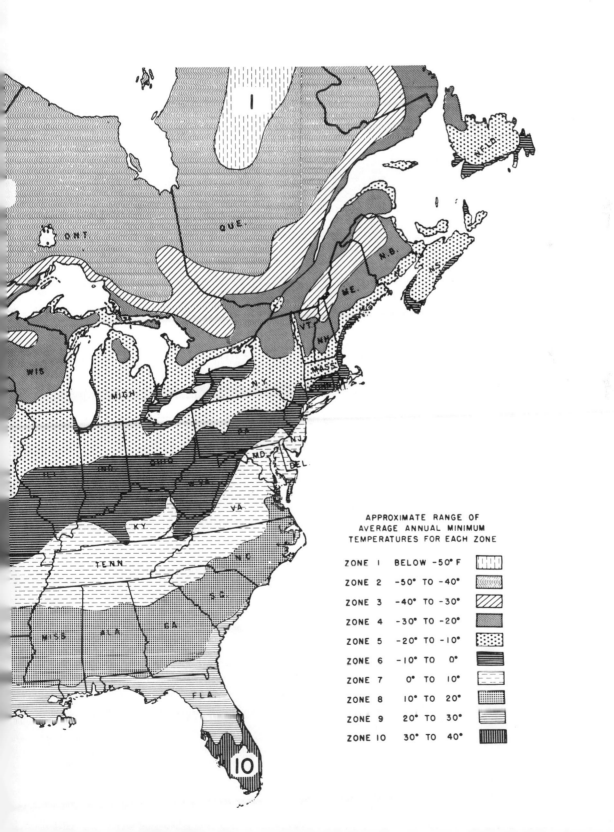

APPROXIMATE RANGE OF
AVERAGE ANNUAL MINIMUM
TEMPERATURES FOR EACH ZONE

ZONE 1   BELOW -50° F
ZONE 2   -50° TO -40°
ZONE 3   -40° TO -30°
ZONE 4   -30° TO -20°
ZONE 5   -20° TO -10°
ZONE 6   -10° TO 0°
ZONE 7   0° TO 10°
ZONE 8   10° TO 20°
ZONE 9   20° TO 30°
ZONE 10   30° TO 40°

D. PLANT AND SEED SOURCES

ORNAMENTAL GRASS PLANTS

Babikow Greenhouses
7838 Babikow Road
Baltimore, MD 21237
301-391-4200

Kurt Bluemel, Inc.
2740 Greene Lane
Baldwin, MD 21013
301-557-7229
Catalog $2

Bluemount Nurseries, Inc.
2103 Blue Mount Road
Monkton, MD 21111
301-329-6226
Wholesale only

Coastal Gardens & Nursery
4611 Socastee Boulevard
Myrtle Beach, SC 29575
803-293-2000
$2 refundable with order

John Greenlee & Associates
301 E. Franklin Avenue
Pomona, CA 91766
714-629-9045

Land Shapes
Rte. 12, Box 144
Lexington, NC 27292
704-249-2010
Wholesale only

Limerock Ornamental Grasses
R.D. 1, Box 111-C
Port Matilda, PA 16870
814-692-2272

Niche Gardens
Rte. 1, Box 290
Chapel Hill, NC 27516
919-967-0078
Catalog $3

Norwood Farms
P.O. Drawer 438
McBee, SC 29101
803-335-6636

Tideland Gardens, Inc.
Chestertown, MD 21620
301-778-5787
Wholesale only

Andre Viette Farm & Nursery
Rte. 1, Box 16
Fishersville, VA 22939
703-943-2315
Catalog $2

Wayside Gardens
Hodges, SC 29695-0001
Catalog $1

EQUISETUM HYEMALE

Sunlight Gardens
Rte. 1, Box 600A
Hillvale Road
Andersonville, TN 37705
(615) 494-8237
Catalog $2

The fields of Limerock Ornamental Grass Nursery in Port Matilda, Pennsylvania.

ORNAMENTAL GRASS SEEDS

W. Atlee Burpee & Co.
Warminster, PA 18974
Annual grass seed

Park Seed Co.
Cokesbury Road
Greenwood, SC 29647-0001

Thompson and Morgan
P.O. Box 1308
Jackson, NJ 08527
1-800-367-7333
Annual and perennial grass seed

NATIVE GRASS PLANTS AND SEEDS

Abundant Life Seed Foundation
P.O. Box 772
Port Townsend, WA 98368
Catalog $1
Seeds of ornamental grasses and corns

Bamert Seed Co.
Rte. 3, Box 1120
Muleshoe, TX 79347
Native grass seed—not less than 5 lb.

Beachley-Hardy Seed Co.
P.O. Box 336
Camp Hill, PA 17011
No mail order
Native grass seed, wildflower and turf seed

Bluebird Nursery, Inc.
P.O. Box 460
Clarkson, NE 68629
Retail on site
Wholesale catalog
No mail order

Ernst Crownvetch Farms
R.D. 5
Meadville, PA 16335
814-425-7276
Seed and plants for reclamation and conservation plantings

Goble Seed Company
P.O. Box 203
Gunnison, UT 84634
Native grass seeds and plants

Grasslander
Chuck & Bev Grimes
Rte. 1, Box 56
Hennessey, OK 73742
Telephone for quote: 405-853-2607
Native grass seeds and plants, custom grass planting, reclamation

High Altitude Gardens
P.O. Box 4238
Ketchum, ID 83340
Seeds, wildflowers
Catalog $2

Idaho Grimm Growers
P.O. Box 276
Blackfoot, ID 83221
Attention: Alan
No mail order
Native grass seed

Johnson Seed Co.
P.O. Box 543
Woodacre, CA 94973
Catalog $1
California native grasses, seeds only

Larner Seeds
P.O. Box 407
Bolinas, CA 94924
415-868-9407
Catalog $1
Seeds, notes on native grasses, design, care

Lafayette Home Nursery, Inc.
R.R. 1, Box 1-A
Lafayette, IL 61449
Plants and seeds
Catalog 50¢

Lofts Seed, Inc.
P.O. Box 146
Bound Brook, NJ 08805
201-356-8700
Native grass seed, wildflower seeds and mixtures

Dwight and Terri Menefee
446 W. Pearson Road #1
Lake Arthur, NM 88253
505-365-2261
No mail order
Hachita blue grama grass

Milaeger's Gardens
4838 Douglas Avenue
Racine, WI 53402-2498
Catalog $1
Native and ornamental grasses

Miller Grass Seed Co., Inc.
7 miles N.E. on Hwy 60
P.O. Box 886
Hereford, TX 79045
Catalog free
Native grasses and wildflowers, seeds

Missouri Wildflowers Nursery
Rte. 2, Box 373
Jefferson City, MO 65101
314-496-3492
Plants and grasses of Missouri, seeds and plants

Native Gardens
Rte. 1, Box 494
(Fisher Lane)
Greenback, TN 37742
615-856-3350
Catalog $1
100% nursery-propagated native perennials, particularly S.E. species, grass plants

Neiman Environments Nursery
2701 Cross Timbers
Flower Mound, TX 75028
Catalog $1
Seeds and plants, wildflower mixtures, environmental restoration services, ornamental grasses, plants and seeds

Northplan Seed Producers
P.O. Box 9107
Moscow, ID 83843
Catalog 50¢ or a large S.A.S.E.
Range and reclamation grasses, many natives

Plants of the Southwest
1812 Second Street
Santa Fe, NM 87501
Catalog $1.50
Native grass seed

Plants of the Wild
Box 866
Tekoa, WA 99033
Catalog $1

Prairie Moon Nursery
Rte. 3, Box 163
Winona, MN 55987
Catalog $1
Native plants and seeds of the driftless area

Prairie Nursery
P.O. Box 365
Westfield, WI 53964
608-296-3679
Catalog $2
Native American prairie wildflowers and grasses: seeds, plants, and landscape
  consultation

Prairie Ridge Nursery
R.R. 2
9738 Overland Road
Mount Horeb, WI 53572-2832
608-437-5245
Catalog 50¢
Native grasses, sedges and wildflowers, consulting and planning service specializing in
  restoring and reconstructing native ecosystems, especially prairies and wetlands.
  Seeds and plants.

Redwood City Seed Co.
P.O. Box 361
Redwood City, CA 94064
List $1 retail, 66¢ wholesale
Native grass seeds and plants, booklets on native grasses, consulting on native
  revegetation—specifically native grasses

Santa Barbara Botanic Garden-Garden Growers
1212 Mission Canyon Road
Santa Barbara, CA 93105
No mail order, grass plants in shop, sometimes native grass seed

Stock Seed Farms, Inc.
Rte. #1, Box 112
Murdock, NE 68407
Native grass seed, wildflowers

Wildflowers from Natures Way
R.R. 1, Box 62
Woodburn, IA 50275
Catalog 25¢ or SASE
Native grass seeds and plants, consulting, management

Winterfield Ranch Seed
Box 97
Swan Valley, ID 83449
Specializing in high-altitude cool-season native grasses and forbs

BAMBOO

A Bamboo Shoot
c/o Richard Waters
1462 Darby Road
Sebastopol, CA 95472
Catalog for business SASE

American Bamboo Company
345 West Second Street
Dayton, OH 45402
Hardy bamboo

David C. Andrews
P.O. Box 10358
Oxon Hill, MD 20745
Free list for business SASE

Bamboo Sourcery
Gerald Bol
666 Wagnon Road
Sebastopol, CA 95472
707-823-5866
Catalog $1

Endangered Species
P.O. Box 1830
Tustin, CA 92681
Free list for business SASE

Frank Hartung Bamboos
10023 14th N.W.
Seattle, WA 98117
Free list for business SASE

L. Helm
Rte. 2, Box 490
Thomson, GA 30824
Free list for business SASE

Northern Groves
3328 S.E. Kelly
Portland, OR 97202
Free catalog for business SASE

Panda Products Nursery
P.O. Box 104
Fulton, CA 95439
Free list for business SASE

Upper Bank Nurseries
P.O. Box 486
Media, PA 19063
Free list for business SASE

Steve Ray's Bamboo Gardens
909 79th Place South
Birmingham, AL 35206
205-833-3052
Catalog $1

Sunset Nursery, Inc.
4007 Elrod Avenue
Tampa, FL 33616
Free list for business SASE

Tradewinds Bamboo Nursery
P.O. Box 70
Calpella, CA 95418
707-485-0835
Free list for business SASE

Tripple Brook Farm
37 Middle Road
Southampton, MA 01073

BIBLIOGRAPHY

Bartram, William. *Travels of William Bartram*, ed. Mark Van Doren. New York: Dover Books, 1928.

Diboll, Neil. "Prairie Plants and Their Use in the Landscape," ed. Steven M. Still, *Proceedings of the 1987 Perennial Plant Symposium*. Baltimore: August, 1987.

Fairchild, David. *The World Was My Garden*. New York and London: Charles Scribner's Sons, 1938.

Farrelly, David. *The Book of Bamboo*. San Francisco: Sierra Club Books, 1984.

Foerster, Karl. *Ein Garten der Errinerung*. Berlin: Union Verlag, 1982.

——————. *Einzug der Graesser und Farne in die Gaerten*. Melsungen, Berlin, Basel, Wien: Verlag J. Neumann-Neudamm, 1957.

Frederick, William H., Jr., and Simon, Richard. "Grass," *Horticulture*, August, 1975.

Galpine, John Kingston. *The Georgian Garden, An Eighteenth-Century Nurseryman's Catalogue*. Stanbridge, Wimborne, Dorset: The Dovecote Press Ltd., 1938.

Gould, Frank W. *Common Texas Grasses*. College Station and London: Texas A&M University Press, 1978.

Grounds, Roger. *Ornamental Grasses*. New York, Cincinnati, Toronto, London, Melbourne: Van Nostrand Reinhold Company, 1979.

Hagemann, H. "Schoene Wintergruene Schattengraeser," *Gartenschoenheit*, Berlin-Westend: February, 1938.

Leighton, Ann. *American Gardens in the Eighteenth Century*. Boston: Houghton Mifflin Company, 1979.

Loewer, H. Peter, *Growing and Decorating with Grasses*. New York: Walker & Company, 1976.

Lowry, Judith. "Notes on Native Design." Bolinas, California: Larner Seeds.

——————. "Notes on Native Grasses." Bolinas, California: Larner Seeds.

Pasture and Range Plants. Bartlesville, Oklahoma: Phillips Petroleum Company, 1963.

Paulus, Heinz. "Von der Arbeit des Gartengestaltes," *Gartenschoenheit*, Berlin-Westend: November, 1938.

Pratt, Anne. *British Grasses and Sedges*. London: Society for Promoting Christian Knowledge, 1859.

Wilson, Ernest H., M.A., V.M.H. *China, Mother of Gardens*. Boston: The Stratford Company, 1929.

INDEX

Boldface page references denote illustrations.

About the Author

Carole Ottesen is a recognized authority and long-time writer on gardening and horticultural design. She attributes her fascination with and love for grasses to the Midwestern prairie landscape of her childhood near Chicago. For most of her adult life, Ms. Ottesen has lived and gardened in the Upper South, near Washington, D.C. She is garden columnist for *Potomac Life Magazine* and a freelance contributor to many publications. She lectures to gardening groups locally and nationwide (including at the National Arboretum) and has taught courses at the USDA Graduate School on horticultural design. Ms. Ottesen is also the author of *The New American Garden,* which was a main selection of the Garden Book Club, and *A Native Plant Primer.*